W9-ADX-147

Finding a Voice While Learning to Teach

*To future teachers and those they will teach,
we wish success in finding a voice.*

*To colleagues and students who helped us find our voices,
we say 'Thank you!'*

Finding a Voice While Learning to Teach

Edited by

Derek Featherstone,
Hugh Munby and Tom Russell

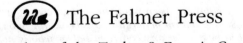 The Falmer Press

(A member of the Taylor & Francis Group)
London • Washington, D.C.

LB2844.1. N4 F56 1997t c.5

UK   The Falmer Press, 1 Gunpowder Square, London, EC4A 3DE
USA   The Falmer Press, Taylor & Francis Inc., 1900 Frost Road, Suite 101, Bristol, PA 19007

© D. Featherstone, H. Munby and T. Russell, 1997

All rights reserved. No part of this publication may be reproduced, stored in a retrieval system, or transmitted in any form or by any means, electronic, mechanical, photocopying, recording or otherwise, without permission in writing from the Publisher.

First published in 1997

A catalogue record for this book is available from the British Library

Library of Congress Cataloging-in-Publication Data are available on request

ISBN 0 7507 0731 3 cased
ISBN 0 7507 0648 1 paper

Jacket design by Caroline Archer

Typeset in 11/13pt Garamond by
Graphicraft Typesetters Ltd., Hong Kong.

Printed in Great Britain by Biddles Ltd, Guildford and King's Lynn on paper which has a specified pH value on final paper manufacture of not less than 7.5 and is therefore 'acid free'.

Every effort has been made to contact copyright holders for their permission to reprint material in this book. The publishers would be grateful to hear from any copyright holder who is not here acknowledged and will undertake to rectify any errors or omissions in future editions of this book.

Contents

Acknowledgments

Most of the anonymous contributions in this collection were prepared by members of a teacher education program operated jointly by the University of Waterloo and Queen's University during their education courses at Queen's in 1994, 1995, and 1996. The editors acknowledge their enthusiasm and support for this type of publication.

Queen's–Waterloo Class of '94

Leo Bacon   Monique Benedetti   Sandy Brownlee   Carolyn Coates
Rob Dickson   Derek Featherstone   Kim Getty   Nadia Gosgnach
Cora Henderson   Robin Kirk   Kristie Laplante   Tim MacLean
Andrea Nichols   Matthew Ott   Maria Paulino   Monica Phillion
Andrea Ricci   Michael Rourke   Shawn Sutcliffe
Cathy Symons   Sandeep Thakrar   Brian Wilhelm

Queen's–Waterloo Class of '95

Jennifer Arnold   Suki Athwal   Marielle Baer   Cristina Batek
Jennifer Bergen   Tracy Charest   Doug Coote   Kevin Godber
Maha Haddad   Sarah Kerr   Brad Kitchen   Amy Meinen
Lianne Nichols   Ian Page   Adam Quast   Leanne Rainbow
Stephanie Sandison   Stacy Schmidt   Krista Schnurr
James Sniatenchuk   Jeff Szeryk   Andy Tsang   David Vrolyk

Queen's–Waterloo Class of '96

John Balfe   Nicole Bradley   Dustin Dickens   Andrea Dyck
Mike Hildebrand   Stacey Honchar   Peter Jensen   Dave Kellow
Geoff Kraemer   Darcy Maguire   Paty Martell   Duncan McIntyre
Colin Muscat   Ray Nassar   Melanie Norton   Steph Parent
Laurie Pistor   Kate Pow   Margaret Ratz   Kevin Smith
Anne Sutton   Heidi Tither   Laura Vander Veen
Shelly Ward   Brian Wilson   Stephanie Wood

Preface

Learning to teach is an exciting, complex, unforgettable experience. Although it often has a formal beginning and end in a university-based program, the informal beginning and end are virtually impossible to define. Our images of teaching go back to our first day at school, or even earlier, and in many respects the experience of learning to teach is never complete.

Experienced teachers, professors of education, and friends and relatives can be very generous with advice about how one should teach, and such advice does have a significant place in learning to teach. This book deliberately emphasizes an alternative source: *finding your own voice* as you learn to teach. More than 80 per cent of the words in this book are written by individuals learning to teach — by individuals who were finding their own voices by writing for themselves, for their fellow beginning teachers, and for those who are following their progress in learning to teach.

We are not the first to recognize that a personal sense of voice can make a significant contribution to the experience of learning to teach, but we believe this is a unique collection of new teachers' voices. Our first audience is others who are learning to teach, but we hope the words of new teachers will also provide useful insights to those who assist new teachers in their entry into the profession.

Derek Featherstone began this project when he was enrolled in education courses, and as we complete it he is in the early months of his second year of teaching at Ashbury College in Ottawa. Derek enrolled in a unique teacher education program operated jointly by Queen's University and the University of Waterloo in Ontario. After four months of teaching in the Fall Term of 1993, he moved immediately to a second four-month period in which he completed all his education courses. In the following year he taught again for four months, and then completed his Bachelor of Science degree. During his education courses in the Winter Term of 1994, he inspired those in his group to join with him to prepare a book about their experiences learning to teach. The two Queen's–Waterloo groups that followed in 1995 and 1996 have also prepared similar books. We are grateful to the members of those groups for permission to reprint some of their writing here.

Hugh Munby and Tom Russell were PhD candidates together at the University of Toronto in 1970–71. Hugh's appointment to the Faculty of Education at Queen's University in Kingston, Ontario, began in 1971, and Tom's followed in 1977. Since 1985 they have collaborated on a program of research that studies the role of reflection-in-learning from experiences of teaching. They are grateful to the Social Sciences and Humanities Research Council of Canada and to the School of Graduate Studies and Research at Queen's University for funding to carry that research forward. They are particularly interested in how individuals understand the *authority* that personal experience provides, and they believe that personal experience has not been recognized adequately as a source of authority. It is here that their research and teaching interests joined with Derek's personal experiences to develop a collection of writing by new teachers who are *finding a voice* while learning to teach.

With the exception of the voice of a third-year teacher in the UK, all the voices presented here are those of individuals learning to teach in Ontario, at Queen's University and the University of Waterloo. The majority of the experiences are set in secondary schools, although there are welcome voices from a few elementary schools. The majority of the secondary school experiences involve the teaching of science, because the individuals experiencing extended teaching placements were in a science option. We believe the voices here will be heard and appreciated by *all* new teachers, beyond our Canadian context and beyond our experiences with secondary science teaching.

We have retained the Ontario-based term of 'associate teacher' to refer to the role that is designated as 'mentor', 'cooperating teacher', 'sponsor teacher', 'associate supervisor' or 'school supervisor' in other jurisdictions in the UK, USA, Australia and Canada. There are numerous references to 'McArthur,' which is the name of the hall in which the Faculty of Education at Queen's is located and thus may be read as a synonym for any college, school or faculty of education. Spelling was a major concern until we elected to leave material in the standard in which it was written. Canadian spelling standards are more 'fluid' than in the UK, the USA, or Australia, but we believe the contributors have been consistent and that meanings will be clear.

We have lost count of the total number of individuals who have contributed voices to this collection, but that does not deny us the opportunity to thank people in groups. The Queen's–Waterloo Concurrent Science Teaching groups who attended courses at Queen's in 1994,

1995, and 1996 inspired our interest in this type of writing and then showed us the way forward. Many members of Tom Russell's Fall 1996 science group gave permission to include some of their in-class writing. Finally, members of the 1996 'pilot project' at Queen's responded quickly to our invitation to enrich this collection with their views on learning to teach. Time and again, we have been encouraged by the positive responses to these invitations to write and to share the results.

We acknowledge the support and participation of Dawn Bellamy, Kevin Smith, and Peter Chin, demonstrated by their contribution of extended accounts of their personal professional development. Tanya Marwitz provided three poems that appear at intervals as a change of pace in the search to understand new teaching experiences. We are grateful to Jan Carrick of Queen's University for much needed assistance in proof-reading. Melissa Ringler and Tanya Marwitz offered valuable editorial suggestions on several sections of the draft manuscript.

We wish to thank Rena Upitis, Dean of Education at Queen's University, for creating an organizational climate that supports innovation, new initiatives, and new teachers' voices. We also thank Roy Napier, Headmaster of Ashbury College, Ottawa, for providing Derek Featherstone's early years of teaching with an environment supportive of professional inquiry and the development of voice.

Introduction

Tom Russell, Derek Featherstone and Hugh Munby

Voice as the Connection between Reflection and Action

Our friend Anna Richert writes eloquently about the significance of voice in learning to teach:

> As teachers talk about their work and 'name' their experiences, they learn about what they know and what they believe. They also learn what they do not know. Such knowledge empowers the individual by providing a source for action that is generated from within rather than imposed from without.... Teachers who know in this way can act with intent; they are empowered to draw from the center of their own knowing and act as critics and creators of their world rather than solely respondents to it, or worse, victims of it. Agency . . . casts voice as the connection between reflection and action. Power is thus linked with agency or intentionality. People who are empowered — teachers in this case — are those who are able to act in accordance with what they know and believe. (Richert, 1992, p. 197)

As we have watched groups of individuals follow different structures for pre-service teacher education at Queen's University in recent years, we have noticed that those who spend more time working in schools and 'learning on the job' tend to be those who have more to say about their teaching experiences, who are more positive about teacher education, and who are more willing to write about and share their experiences of learning to teach. This volume brings together a range of material illustrating the development of voice by those learning to teach. The collection begins with shorter pieces that illustrate the range of experiences that a new teacher encounters and examines. Longer pieces of writing follow to reveal details of the development of several individuals learning to teach. From time to time, the editors insert brief comments to indicate the meanings that they see in specific passages. One of our goals is to keep our own words to a minimum, to help live our belief that the voices of new teachers deserve to be a central focus of pre-service teacher education.

Structures for teacher education programs are numerous, representing many variations on the standard theme: Time in university-based courses alternates with classroom teaching placements of varying lengths. Many teacher education programs begin and end in the university classroom, with teaching practice in several settings sprinkled throughout. This could be characterized as a model in which 'theories, maxims and rules of thumb' are learned at university and then 'put into practice' in a school classroom. We hope that readers who are enrolled in a program following this model will find the range of material here to be helpful in anticipating the practicum experience and in making sense of it afterwards. Certainly, the experiences described here will take on more and more meaning as the reader acquires personal experiences of teaching.

As we complete our editing of this collection, the Faculty of Education at Queen's University is conducting a 'pilot' version of a new program structure for pre-service teacher education. One key feature of the new structure is 'early extended teaching experience' — four months of teaching that begin on the first day of the school year in September and continue until the holiday break in December. This structure assumes that those learning to teach can play a significant teaching role without formal instruction first, and that they do so by drawing on their personal stores of images of how teachers and students interact in classrooms. With an experienced teacher to guide and support their initial lessons, the new structure assumes that a teacher candidate's 'on-the-job learning' will provide insights into the previously inaccessible ways in which teachers think about their work, generating a range of questions and issues that will inform the courses that follow at the university. Chapter 5 of this book presents the voices of several individuals participating in the 'pilot project' that is preparing the way for the first full offering of the new program in 1997–98.

Voice as the Connection between Experience and Authority

Voice is the connection between *reflection and action*, as Richert suggests. Voice can also be seen as the connection between *experience and authority*. As people learning to teach gain experience, they also gain confidence, yet this confidence at the practical level does not always translate directly into what might be called 'professional confidence.' We (Munby and Russell, 1994) have developed a view that giving authority to one's personal experience while learning to teach is *central* to understanding how and what one is learning from experience.

Quite naturally, new teachers place high value on the authority of experienced teachers' voices, particularly with respect to 'what works and what doesn't work.' New teachers also realize that people based in universities have much to offer them, although the authority of 'theory and research' often ranks much lower in the eyes of new teachers for the very obvious reason that what they do 'must work — now, not later.' Both groups of individuals derive their authority from their experience and they do their best to share those experiences in ways that will be valuable to new teachers.

The obvious respect that new teachers grant to experienced teachers may be the most obvious reason why new teachers tend not to grant themselves enough authority to add their own voices to the experiences of teacher education and the early years of teaching. The first year of teaching is universally exhausting and demanding, and none should be surprised if that experience reduces the new teacher's respect for the pre-service preparation that typically precedes the first year. If one's preparation is in doubt and one has been overwhelmed by the first year of experience, one is not likely to grant much personal authority to oneself.

We believe that it is only too easy for new teachers and pre-service teacher candidates to 'sell themselves short,' and that encouraging the development of voice can counter this tendency. We rejoice in the quality of the voices in this collection and in the enthusiasm shown time and again by individuals and groups of new teachers for developing and sharing their voices with others. Thus we believe that the initial preparation of teachers will only improve as we show new teachers how to develop a personal sense of voice and authority and then support them by listening to their voices. They have years of experience as students, years that developed a large storehouse of images of what teachers do and don't do. These images are one strand of their personal, experienced-based authority. Then, as they begin to teach and meet directly the behind-the-scenes thinking of a teacher, their very earliest experiences convey an important sense of authority. This authority is delicate and fragile, but, as this collection demonstrates, it can sustain a voice if given the opportunity. We hope that the voices presented here will encourage new teachers everywhere to set their own voices alongside those of experienced teachers and teacher educators, taking the time to draw appropriately on each as the basis for personally-directed, career-long professional learning.

The Plan of the Book

Chapters 1, 2 and 3 in this collection are designed to set the stage for all that follows, by introducing some of the common themes and concerns of individuals approaching their earliest teaching assignments. Led by Derek Featherstone's voice, the editors provide a simple structure for presentation of many new-teacher voices. We believe these chapters will be valuable reading before and during the earliest weeks of a teaching placement.

Chapters 4, 5 and 6 are intended to move forward the process of learning from experience in a teaching placement. Chapter 4 illustrates a range of responses to three weeks of teaching, while Chapter 5 provides responses based on eight weeks of teaching. Both chapters are relevant to learning from teaching experience, while the contrast between the two chapters begins to indicate the effects of a longer assignment. Chapter 6 reveals the voices of individuals who began teaching with only a few days of orientation as they looked back after four months later to consider the issue of 'Am I really ready to teach?' — a question that many experienced teachers still ask themselves the night before a new school year begins.

Chapters 7 and 8 provide single voices speaking at length about learning to teach. In Chapter 7, Kevin Smith describes the crises he endured as he moved from his initial expectation that he would learn to teach by being told the moves, to a final conclusion that experience is the most appropriate teacher. In Chapter 8, Dawn Bellamy provides an account of her continuing struggle to develop voice and confidence during her pre-service program and her first two years of teaching.

Chapters 9 and 10 return the spotlight to Derek Featherstone, whose voice in the first three chapters speaks to the nature of the experiences of individuals seeking teacher certification. In these closing chapters, the nature of Derek's development in his first and second year of teaching offers invitations to other new teachers to assume personal responsibility for their own professional development. In Chapter 9, Derek describes his efforts to show his science students how to develop their own voices in ways that will inform his teaching. In Chapter 10, Derek's 'trialogue' with Peter Chin and Tom Russell shows how discussions of teaching can continue after certification, to the benefit of both teachers and teacher educators.

Several chapters begin with an 'Overview' set in a smaller font to indicate that it is explanatory material provided by the editors as a guide to the voices that constitute the main body of the chapter.

Related Literature

Before handing the microphone and spotlight to those learning to teach, we wish to identify several pieces of related literature that have supported and encouraged the development of this collection. We recommend them highly to those who are learning to teach, and to those who have the privilege of working with new teachers. The two 'senior members' of this editing trio began to focus on the authority that comes with experience in a paper titled, 'The authority of experience in learning to teach: Messages from a physics methods course' (Munby and Russell, 1994). By using the voices of teacher candidates to describe various issues that arise in the pre-service teacher education experience, we began to realize the power of new teachers' voices in the development of teacher education. That publication appeared just as Derek Featherstone (the 'junior member' of the trio, but certainly not the junior voice) was leading his cohort of Queen's–Waterloo science teachers to publish their voices in the collection that inspired *Finding a Voice While Learning to Teach*.

The voices of individuals learning to teach are made apparent in very significant ways in *Becoming a Student of Teaching* (Bullough and Gitlin, 1995) and *Through Preservice Teachers' Eyes* (Knowles, Cole, and Presswood, 1994). When a new teacher is ready to move beyond these valuable guides, we recommend *Becoming a Critically Reflective Teacher* (Brookfield, 1995) as a unique source of ideas and perspectives for sustaining personal development as a teacher.

Just as this collection presents the voices of those learning to teach, we are also seeing collections that present the voices of those who teach those learning to teach. When a teacher candidate or new teacher is ready to look 'behind the scenes' into the world of teacher education itself, we recommend the following titles, also available from Falmer Press. *Teachers Who Teach Teachers: Reflections on Teacher Education* (Russell and Korthagen, 1995) and *Teaching about Teaching: Purpose, Passion and Pedagogy in Teacher Education* (Loughran and Russell, 1997) are edited collections that present a range of views about the forces that inspire and sustain teacher educators. *Opening the Classroom Door: Teacher, Researcher, Learner* (Loughran and Northfield, 1996) is a compelling account of the issues and emotions that arose during and after an experienced teacher educator's year-long return to classroom teaching.

References

BROOKFIELD, S.D. (1995) *Becoming a Critically Reflective Teacher*, San Francisco, Jossey-Bass.

BULLOUGH, R.V., JR. and GITLIN, A. (1995) *Becoming a Student of Teaching: Methodologies for Exploring Self and School Context*, New York, Garland.

KNOWLES, J.G., COLE, A.L. and PRESSWOOD, C. (1994) *Through Preservice Teachers' Eyes: Exploring Field Experiences through Narrative and Inquiry*, New York, Merrill.

LOUGHRAN, J. and NORTHFIELD, J. (1996) *Opening the Classroom Door: Teacher, Researcher, Learner*, London, Falmer Press.

LOUGHRAN, J. and RUSSELL, T. (eds) (1997) *Teaching about Teaching: Purpose, Passion and Pedagogy in Teacher Education*, London, Falmer Press.

MUNBY, H. and RUSSELL, T. (1994) 'The authority of experience in learning to teach: Messages from a physics methods course', *Journal of Teacher Education*, **45**, 2, pp. 86–95.

RICHERT, A.E. (1992) 'Voice and power in learning to teach', in VALLI, L. (ed.) *Reflective Teacher Education: Cases and Critiques*, Albany, NY, State University of New York.

RUSSELL, T. and KORTHAGEN, F. (eds) (1995) *Teachers Who Teach Teachers: Reflections on Teacher Education*, London, Falmer Press.

Chapter 1

Learning to Teach:
The Learning Is *in* the Experience

Others Cannot Tell You, but They Can Help

Major goals of this book include helping pre-service and beginning teachers to recognize their important role in education, showing them how to better understand their journey of becoming a teacher, and — as a result — *finding a voice* that will carry them confidently into a challenging *and* rewarding career. The following words, written by a pre-service teacher during education courses, capture the essence and the purpose of this book:

> Who among us really knows what it means to teach? I'll tell you who knows — those who have taught long enough to realize that they really don't know anything compared to how much there is to learn about teaching. You can never stop learning. One thing that I've learned about teaching is that experience is the only 'true' teacher.
>
> This book cannot teach you how to teach, your professors can't teach you, your mother can't teach you, and we certainly can't teach you. We can guide you, but we can't tell you what to do in every possible situation. Like teaching, learning to teach is a very personal experience, and we hope you will enjoy letting the many voices collected here guide your learning to teach.
>
> Everyone will handle different situations differently; some may be handled better than others, but ultimately the choice is yours to make. The only way that one can learn to teach is by actually teaching. So maybe the question should be, 'What does teaching involve?' Well, to me, it involves getting up each morning, looking at myself in the mirror, saying 'Damn, I'm late again!', running to school, going nuts in the classroom because students keep shoving things into the gas valve outlets (or trying to smack each other around when I'm not looking), working late at nights, being frustrated, working hard, being exhausted . . . and still loving it all . . . because of that one student in the corner who is trying his absolute very best but who never succeeds (and it burns me to see that) but then he finally does succeed, and then that awesome feeling comes over me because I can see that

he's got a feeling that is just as awesome, and a smile creeps onto both our faces.

Teaching's most satisfying moments tend to be those when a teacher 'connects' with a student and makes a difference to that individual. Similarly, learning to teach is a unique and personal journey. We hope that you will 'connect' with many people as you learn to teach. While others cannot tell you how to teach, they can help you find your way, helping you to develop a sense of voice as you make that journey. Writing about your experiences and then sharing those experiences — not only with experienced teachers and professors but also with others making the same journey — is the theme of this book and a process central to finding your way as a new teacher.

Teaching Is a Personal Enterprise

Consider the following case, and ask yourself whether someone really could have told this pre-service teacher what to do, before this class began. It may not have made a difference when the teacher was actually experiencing the situation. Teaching is a personal enterprise. Yes, other educators can tell you about classroom management problems, and they may be able to give you tips and strategies for success, but without your own experiences to think about and relate to, is that *really* learning? Is it learning that will be available to you on the spur of the moment, in the middle of a lesson? Or is it more like memorizing procedures that really don't make sense to you? Is it largely algorithmic, where stimulus A leads to response 1 and stimulus B leads to response 2?

> During one class, many of the students were talking and being very uncooperative while I was trying to explain a very important concept to them. I was working really hard to make them understand. After repeated attempts to settle the class I put out the warning that if they didn't settle down I would be forced to eject those who were being disruptive from the room. This threat was enough for most students, but not for all. A few persisted in their behaviour, not heeding my warning. The student who was being most disruptive was Mary, so naturally she was to be removed from the class first. I said, 'Mary, would you please leave the room?' Mary replied, 'No, I don't want to.'
>
> The tone of her voice was not one of defiance but rather one of genuine desire to stay in the classroom. Having issued a request, I was not about to let it go unnoticed. Again I asked if she would leave the room, this time more firmly, and again she refused, saying, 'No, I don't

want to miss today's notes.' I now noticed that all the other students were now watching intensely what was going on between Mary and myself. With as much strength as I could put behind my voice I said, 'Mary, leave the room.' I was no longer asking but ordering. Mary, now quite defiant, simply said 'No.' I could see now that Mary wasn't going to budge. I could not ask again. I didn't want to remove her physically and I didn't want to involve the administration or other teachers, so I said as quietly as I could, 'I will see you after class.'

Over a 30-second period, Mary had taken away what little respect and authority I had with the class. With all the tension in the air, nobody dared misbehave for the rest of the period, but this was not the way I wanted to achieve this behaviour. After class had finished I had a long talk with Mary. I did not disguise that I had been very hurt and disappointed by her behaviour nor did I neglect to tell her all of the implications of it. I explained to her how she had taken away much of my credibility. How could I enforce any of my rules if the other students knew that I could not or would not enforce them? Mary tried to justify her actions by saying that I was not being fair since others were also misbehaving, or that I was only picking on her because she was a girl. She agreed with me that my tactics were fair for other students, and that she was behaving in a manner that befitted the punishment, but she refused to accept that she should have been sent from the classroom. A debate ensued, and when it was over, neither of us had succeeded in changing the other's stance. After our meeting I could tell that she also had been very hurt by the experience.

A meeting with her mother a week later, during parent–teacher interviews, confirmed my impressions. Mary had been quite disturbed by the situation. Although our relationship did re-establish itself in a few days, I sensed that something was just a bit different between us.

Teaching Is about Making Differences to Individuals

Discipline is always a major concern for those of us learning to teach. Experienced teachers *seem* to handle discipline so easily. They can tell us what they would do or would have done, but usually they cannot tell us how they know what to do in a given situation. Once we gain confidence in dealing with the day-to-day routine of managing a class, we may be able to accomplish some wonderful things. We all dream of being that 'special teacher' for a troubled student, and the following account shows that achieving that dream can happen to beginners.

I will always remember Ryan for his stake in my learning how to teach. Here was a student I had from Day 1. Although he hadn't been tested, he fit the description of a boy with attention deficit disorder (ADD). I've tutored a few students diagnosed with ADD, and Ryan had many behavioral similarities to them. Every day he'd make himself known to the class by creating some kind of problem. It was very difficult for him to sit still. Near the end of the term I learned that his other teachers had been giving him detentions all term, and in my final week at the school he was suspended. On some days he tried his hardest to get himself kicked out of my class, but I wouldn't budge on my decision not to kick students out. He taught me patience, and how to incorporate problem behaviour into a lesson. Throughout my teaching there, Ryan made remarkable progress.

I'll never forget the look he gave me one day after a test. The class was writing a unit test and Ryan hadn't studied, so it took him 3 minutes to write it. I knew I'd have a problem on my hands if I didn't get him to do some quiet seat work. I took him to the side room and asked him if he wanted to do well in my class. He said he would but didn't know how and didn't keep the notes. I told him he could make a fresh start by doing the homework in the next unit and, if he wanted, he could come in the mornings or at lunch and I would help him organize notes from earlier lessons, and I would let him rewrite the tests, but only if he showed me he was committed.

I started him off on the homework, which was going to be given out after the test. He had never before worked so diligently in my class. After 25 minutes, without a peep or even looking up from his book, he came to ask me some questions. I said, 'Ryan, you are really doing well. Keep it up and you'll definitely pass. This is good work.' He looked at me with a big smile on his face and a look in his eyes as though no one had ever told him that before. He went straight back to his desk and worked quietly. After class he said that he wanted to do better and asked if I really thought he could. I had every confidence in him that he could and I let him know that.

The next class brought an amazing improvement. He had done the homework, and so he had something to contribute and he would put up his hand. He even admonished other students who didn't have their homework done by saying, 'If you just sat down and did it, it wouldn't take long. Besides it wasn't hard anyway!' I couldn't believe that Ryan gave the rest of the class a kick in the pants! He said he would try to finish homework and that the hardest thing for him to stop doing was talking. He certainly tried. He put his hand up when I asked questions and even put it back down quietly when I didn't call on him. He came in before classes to get help with putting his notebook in order and he also came in at lunch for help. He really impressed me with his change in behaviour. He wanted to know why I wanted to help him and candidly said that no one bothered to treat him nicely as I did.

I couldn't believe it when I heard it! What did all his other teachers do? No wonder he came in with that attitude. But thanks to patience and perseverance, he was able to see that the classroom atmosphere allowed for his opinions and that he could approach me about anything he wanted. His quizzes and homework checks revealed the amount of work he was putting in. He came in early almost every morning and also came in at lunch for help. He never expected that individual attention during class and finally learned the behaviour I found to be acceptable.

Sadly, he didn't put that effort forth in the rest of his classes and he saved most of his outbursts for them. In the lunch room, Ryan's name came up quite frequently, in not-so-good terms. I couldn't believe these experienced teachers couldn't see through his act — his test. The principal commented that it surprised him that I never assigned Ryan's name to detention hall or sent him to the office. I didn't know that was what I was *expected* to do.

Cases such as this are challenging in many different ways. We are pleased that it shows a new teacher making a difference to a student. But not every new teacher achieves such dramatic success in such an apparently straightforward manner. And in the end, the success was bittersweet, when Ryan was unable to behave differently in other classes and ultimately left the school. Not all teachers could reach Ryan. While youth and fresh perspective may have helped one person make a difference for Ryan, a more experienced teacher might have been able to create a network of others who shared that perspective and then used it to keep Ryan in the school. Making a difference is usually very complex.

At the same time, the story of Ryan captures some of the reasons that help beginning teachers decide to enter the teaching profession. The words of the story also highlight some of the features of any teaching experience. Statements such as, 'I didn't know that was what I was expected to do,' are not uncommon from pre-service teachers or from experienced teachers. It can be particularly troublesome to see a student or a class in your own way, only to find that others are seeing a quite different picture. You will find that there *are* others who see things much as you do, and you will also find that there are others whose perspectives are ones that you need. Finding such people and the time to engage them is a major challenge in the profession of teaching, as in many others. Knowing that you are 'not the only one' can be a great relief.

Finally, writing about Ryan has helped one new teacher make substantial progress in finding a professional voice. As we read the story, the substantial investment made by one person on Ryan's behalf emerges loudly and clearly. By creating such an account, the author has demonstrated commitment to students and also to teaching. And exercising one's voice in such a written account produces a 'paper trail' that documents the professional learning experience, for the benefit of the individual and also for the benefit of those with whom such accounts may be shared.

Learning to Teach Is a Personal Journey

Perhaps teacher education programs should be designed with sharing in mind, so that a community of teachers can be established in which we share our experiences, both positive and negative, and support each other in our entry into the profession. Perhaps faculties of education are already like that. Perhaps their function is to allow beginning teachers to be part of a group in which many people are feeling the same stresses and are puzzling over the same types of issues. Perhaps the difference lies in pre-service teachers' perceptions of the function of a school or faculty of education.

Although subtle, there is a difference between wanting to be taught and wanting to learn, and it may make an incredible difference in how people approach their professional program. If you want to be 'taught,' then perhaps you want to be told what to do, how to do it, when to do it, where to do it, and who to do it to. If you want to 'learn' (with the help of others), then perhaps you want to share experiences and thoughts with others so that you can evaluate for yourself what might work for you and how it might fit into your own teaching style.

> In my first four months of teaching on my practicum, I must admit that I was really eased slowly into this demanding role. Many of the teachers in the science department were quite young and had obviously not forgotten the scariness of this first 'immersion.' I began solely as a classroom helper, and spent most of my time observing and helping students one-on-one, feeling out my new position, gaining confidence in even just talking with the students. This initial nervousness left me pretty quickly and it was not long before I was very comfortable, even happy in this role. To this day, my favourite part of my teaching experience has been working one-on-one with the students. A little bit to my horror, this 'comfort' became obvious to my associates and they invited me to take another step. So there I was again, stripped of my confidence, having to redefine my role in the classroom. Of course, in my nervous state, my first lesson was a whirlwind that left the students' hair ruffled. I am a very harsh judge of myself, and I went home

convinced that I was not the right person for this job. The next few weeks and months, I was set on a road to rebuild my self-confidence as a teacher. I had felt pretty confident in front of that full-length mirror, in those fancy shoes, teaching my 3-year-old sister and her imaginary classmates. The real thing, I was realizing, was a different slice.

Getting to know the students in my classes from a teacher's perspective, learning their needs, their pace, and their ways of communicating to me eventually smoothed out many of the wrinkles. Yet I was never sure that I was 'doing the right thing,' interpreting and playing my part correctly, so I found that I was never really totally at ease. That was precisely the reason I was looking forward to my education courses at Queen's. There they would tell me the answers to my questions and I would leave with the knowledge I would need to be a good teacher. Well, you can imagine my horror when I discovered that I was to spend a big chunk of my time in small-group discussions with other novices, still as wet behind the ears as I was. I was thinking, 'Where the heck has all my money gone?' I could have gone to the pub for free and had the chance to talk about my experiences with these people. I wanted experts. WHERE WERE MY EXPERTS???

My views of this Faculty of Education have softened as I have come to the realization that my experts are with me, and they are doing a wise thing in allowing me to explore my own answers to my own questions by herding me gently into circles with others who have experienced much the same. And these wise experts have not just left us to ourselves, for they have challenged us to take a different view, to question what exactly makes a good teacher and to question what and why we are teaching. This has been yet another new role I have had to adjust to and it has again taken time for me to regain my confidence. But of the questions raised here, many have not yet been answered, and perhaps my full confidence will not be gained until such time as they are. If, as I suspect, some of these questions will never be answered or their answers will need redefining every once in a while, I will never be totally comfortable or satisfied with my interpretation of the part I have to play. This I now see as a positive thing, as the slight uneasiness will keep me on a search, forever redefining and refining myself. All this has fallen nicely into a phrase I have heard somewhere before within these walls: *the moment a teacher ceases to learn, that teacher begins to die.*

Answers versus questions. Absolutes versus maybes. Well-defined black and white versus hazy shades of grey. Others cannot tell you how to teach, but they *can* help you to understand the journey as they also help you find your way and as you find a professional voice.

Everyone knows that you must 'stand up and teach' as part of the process of learning to teach and being certified to teach. We often speak, casually, in terms of *having* experience and then asking what we learned *from* experience, as though the two are separate, logically and chronologically. As you continue through this collection of new teachers' voices, we urge you to consider that experience and learning are a single process — the learning is *in* the experience. Developing a voice is a way of acknowledging the authority of experience-based learning.

Chapter 2

Common Themes in Learning to Teach

Overview

In this chapter, Derek Featherstone provides the introduction and connecting narrative for a series of themes related to new teachers finding common ground in their teaching experiences as part of building a community of teacher–learners. While many of the voices heard in this chapter relate to classroom management and ownership, the themes also include the unpredictability of teaching and the issue of loneliness in a practice teaching assignment.

I'm Not the Only One Who Feels This Way

I can recall the sense of relief I felt when I arrived at Queen's University in January, 1994 for my formal education coursework. My classmates and I had just finished a strenuous four-month period of teaching in secondary schools, with the guidance and supervision of teachers. I knew that I was not left alone for that time — I had help from other teachers in the school that I was working at — but somehow it was not quite enough. It was comforting in some respects to at least have someone to talk to about my experiences, but, at the same time, most of the teachers who were willing to discuss things with me were more experienced than I, and they were quite a long way away (at least in my mind) from their own student teaching experiences. How could they possibly know what I was feeling? How could they possibly know what I was going through? How could they possibly understand my problems? They couldn't! They could relate it to their own experiences several years earlier, but they were not at the same career stage and thus I thought they could have quite easily 'forgotten' what it was like to be a pre-service teacher. I should make it clear that I do not hold them at fault for this. They were always willing to help me in any way they could. Their support and kind ears were most appreciated.

What I am talking about here is something different. One reason that I enjoyed the first weeks of my education courses so much was the validation and relief that I felt when I discovered that I was not the only one experiencing problems and having successes in the classroom. I know that I was not physically isolated during my first teaching experiences, but at times I felt mentally and emotionally isolated. I needed to hear other pre-service teachers' stories of what they had gone through. It was a metaphorical 'shoulder to cry on' that might have helped me during my first teaching term. Perhaps it would have been even better if that shoulder belonged to teachers in the same stage of their career, who might better understand what I was feeling.

Knowing that I was not the only one was important to me. I was not a failure. Others were having problems too. Most people have a predisposition to worry that they are not 'normal' (whatever that is). Hearing others' stories and offering my own helped to remove the sometimes sharp pain of feeling inadequate as a teacher. It helped me feel normal. Other pre-service teachers were searching for answers to some of the same questions, and some helped me to realize other questions that I might not have seen before. Is that what a community of pre-service teachers learning together could be all about?

If I felt isolated and wished that I had someone at the same stage as myself to talk to, is it not reasonable to assume that others might feel something similar? But what if there is nobody to have a conversation with? Perhaps you feel the need to talk to someone else from outside the institution where you are teaching. It is not uncommon that there be only one pre-service teacher in a school, but even if there *is* more than one, the demands of teaching create such busy schedules that there may be little hope in coordinating a time when you can get together. So who can you talk to that understands what you are feeling, doing and experiencing?

With this question in mind, I made it one of my objectives in writing for and co-editing this book to create a piece of work that helps to address the distress and potential isolation that pre-service teachers can feel. If you have nobody to turn to, we hope that you might turn to this book as you begin to teach. We hope that it will reassure you that you are not alone, and that you are not the only one. In a way, we are hoping that you might be able to have, for the lack of a better word, a 'conversation' with this book. We hope that one-way conversation is better than no conversation at all. And, if you do have someone to talk to or you are in education courses right now, then reading parts of this book may serve to rekindle memories of experiences that you may want to discuss, either privately or in classes. Included below are a number of short pieces of writing, grouped into common themes, to give glimpses into the myriad of experiences in teaching.

The Unexpected

Teaching is unpredictable. Sometimes things seem to pop up from no-where to simply 'blow you away.' Sometimes your best intentions can backfire completely, leaving you in a quandary. And even if someone had told you that a certain type of event might happen, it doesn't really 'hit home' until it happens to you. In the first of five voices included in this section about the unexpected events of teaching, a teacher candidate deals with a student who has a dramatic strategy for avoiding going to class.

On my way to Grade 10 science class, I was stopped by Melanie and dragged into a side room (the 'entrance' to the vice-principal's office) and she told me she just needed to talk. She started to bawl. Great. What the hell am I going to do here? I have to get to class and help Mark (my associate teacher), but I also have a girl breaking down on me. I stayed with her, and let her explain what was going on — she was crying like you wouldn't believe, and was barely fitting in time to breathe. I could only help so much, and I really felt like I was getting nowhere with her. I almost felt guilty because, for a large part of the time I was with her, I was thinking about what I could do to get myself to the class I was supposed to be with. What would I have done if I were a full-time teacher, and Mark had not been there to handle the rest of the class? There is no way that class could have been left alone for the length of time I was dealing with Melanie!

It was brutal, and I couldn't help feeling that I had no idea where this kid was coming from — her problems definitely went far beyond what I'll ever see yet I felt I needed to help. I don't think I could ever turn away a student (or any person for that matter . . .) who came to me crying, asking for help. Eventually I got her calmed down. As soon as I asked her if she wanted to go do her work in the library, she seemed to be a lot better. Her main concern all along was having to go to science and face Catherine (her best friend who was apparently not talking to her any more). She took the crossword puzzle that I had made up for the class, and went to the library to work. I felt a little better about what was going on, but still felt horrible for leaving Mark on his own with those twenty-four others. I went there right away, and told him what had happened, and he said, 'Well, that sounds like par for the course.' Apparently she does this on a regular basis. I felt like a sucker. Maybe I didn't get sucked in (Mark agrees that this is a possibility). Maybe she will be a little better tomorrow.

* * * * *

The following paragraph reminds us that students' 'personal problems' are very real to them. All the wishing in the world cannot make personal problems go away or deny their relevance to each individual's ability to function 'normally' in a classroom.

> In my school there were at least twenty girls who were pregnant. Seeing these children having children themselves was a reality check for me. I had one girl in my Grade 9 class who turned from being a well-behaved young girl to someone I constantly had to tell to be quiet. She was going through some major mood swings and her grades were being affected. I went to guidance to see if they knew what was happening with her and all they would tell me was she was having 'personal problems.' I could not think of anything that could make this girl change so much and then, after pursuing it further, I found that she was afraid she was pregnant. She was frightened and acted the only way she knew how to in order to forget how scared she was. A lot of young girls have to deal with this now and as teachers we have to have enough compassion to help them through this. Singling her out and reprimanding her would have only made things worse.

* * * * *

Experienced teachers can recommend that you not let students 'get away with little things', but that good advice only works when we have learned how to recognize little things as requiring our attention. This voice tells how the relationship with one student 'escalated' into one that could not be neglected, and it also shows the importance of relying on other teachers as well as those who have a school-wide view of a student's behaviour.

> The hardest moment, and one of the best learning experiences I had, was when a student started harassing me. Let me explain. Throughout the first few weeks of teaching a Grade 10 class, a student started making inappropriate remarks. They seemed harmless at first although they made me uncomfortable since I wasn't sure how to take them. The problem was, the remarks were so subtle that it was hard to tell if the insult was intentional or not. Anyway, the remarks started getting a little more blatant (for example, he told his seat mate, 'Boy, you sure smell today!'). I took him aside after class and we discussed the inappropriate remarks he had been making. He seemed apologetic, but in the first few minutes of class the next day, he came up to me

and said, 'I don't like your attitude today.' At precisely that moment my associate walked in. He didn't hear what was said but saw the exchange and knew the history. This time he took the student aside and spoke with him. Apparently, the student was given a choice: to either stop the remarks or spend some class time in the office. The student returned to class and proceeded to make three or four more comments. Not wanting to start an argument in class, which I'm sure he wanted, I didn't react. So, he instead gave me the finger. I still didn't react, but after class my associate and I visited the vice-principal. The student had been given several warnings and had just gotten worse, and he received a two-day in-school suspension. I later found out he had a history of giving teachers problems, especially when he thought he could get away with it — for instance when having a student teacher. The thing that I learned is not to let anything go. If I had spoken with the student right at the beginning instead of trying to remain 'cool,' perhaps the situation wouldn't have escalated.

* * * * *

The following passage is a response to a formal exercise asking teacher candidates to recall a 'day one' situation that challenged them to re-think their assumptions and then explain what happened in the next class, on 'day two'. While most responses give a positive account of day two, it is no surprise that this account of a negative experience de-scribes unexpected events in managing a diverse group of students.

It was a Grade 11 environmental science class comprised of students that school didn't always agree with, but they liked the teacher who taught the course. This was a teacher who was never sick, except for this week. I had taught the class once before as a supply teacher, but now I had them for a week. Monday rolled around and the class was great; they got on with their work, and they seemed to enjoy what they were doing. The second day they were pretty good, but they started to get restless near the end of the class. To fill up time I decided to show them a video, and that was my big mistake. I insisted that the students be reasonably quiet during the video, and one of the class ringleaders decided to use this as a power struggle. I sent him to the office, which made him mad and triggered what was to follow. It must be noted that in this class there were about fifteen cool kids, and three misfits. Two of the misfits were really nice guys who, after being out in the workforce for about 12 years, had decided to come back to school. The third day was disaster. Most of the class started to pick on the misfits, and were quite ruthless. I should have stopped it when it began, but I was too slow, and I let the first few shots from the back of the class slip by. Unknown to me some of the guys at the back of the class were shooting spitballs into the hair of the older guys. Not impressed by this, one of the 'targets' went into a rage, threatening to smash a chair over the head of one of the trouble-makers. The chair was up and ready for action before he cooled down enough to just leave the room. Pandemonium ensued, and I knew I had lost control of the class. The rest of the week was a living night-mare, one I don't want to repeat. That is the end of my day one/day two odyssey into the dark side.

* * * * *

As one is getting to know a student who is 'having problems', it is only natural to make assumptions that can later be seen as incorrect. The author of this complex account of his personal disappointment with his own unexpected response in a meeting does not give himself credit for the fact that he faced the complex task of learning to interact with a parent and with other teachers in the important professional exercise of combining perspectives to understand a situation better and develop a common course of action.

I had my first parents' meeting on Tuesday night. We all sat down and met as teachers with one student's parents, and I came away from that meeting with a completely new perspective on what goes on in the life of some children. My main purpose for going was so that I could get a head start on working with this student. (I will be working with him for a three-week block that began yesterday.) Although I wanted to form my own opinions of him and give him a clean slate, in a case where there is significant background information that would help me in my working with the students, I want to know. It was smart of me to go to the meeting. We went around the table discussing this stu-dent's abilities and the problems that each teacher saw as getting in the way of his learning. I must stress here how much I hated this exercise. As I listened to the other teachers, I felt absolutely horrible. Very few nice things were said about J and I noticed that J's mother was having a very difficult time talking about what was happening to her son. J's year was in jeopardy. This is his second time through Grade 9. He already feels 'behind' socially, because all of his friends are in Grade 10. (Later in the meeting, the principal said something to the effect that, whatever happens, J will not be repeating Grade 9 again — i.e., social promotion.)

Where am I to go with this? I think that J is in real trouble. When it was my turn to speak about J, all I could say was that I was there to try and get some insight into what was going on and how I could best help J in the three weeks that I have him. (In the four months I was teaching this course, a new group of students rotated to my associate and me every three weeks.) I caught myself saying something that triggered me to think about not only what I had just said but also how I had said it. I felt horrible after the meeting. I said, 'I've only had J in class for two days, and today he didn't show up.' His mother replied that he was at home, sick, and that she knew about it. I felt horrible, and to be honest, I don't think anyone picked up on what I had said or how I had said it other than J's mom. Why did I say that he 'didn't show up'? I said it because I assumed from what I had heard that J was the type who would skip classes. I know it is a little thing, but sometimes it is the little things that bug me most — obviously this one stuck out in my mind! I would have preferred to have said that J 'was absent today', and not have this attitude in my head that he was skipping. I think I picked this attitude up from some other teachers and I wish this incident had never happened. One of the main reasons it bugs me is that the mother was so quick to defend her child to me. She knew he was at home, sick, and she really put me in my place. I felt small and weak, and I was sweating.

These accounts are not role plays or imaginary scenarios. They are real stories of real experiences that happened to real people learning to teach. Is it possible to expect the unexpected? If it were, would it make a difference? It is impossible to figure out exactly what will go wrong before it does.

Classroom Management

It is not just pre-service teachers who cannot predict what will happen in their classes. All teachers have to deal with the inherent unpredictability of teaching. One of the most common areas of unforeseen events is classroom management. The stories included below are typical situations that occur in classrooms. They are told by those they happened to, and include their thoughts on what they might do differently in a similar situation if it were to arise again. The first of eleven voices included in this section on classroom management issues and situations deals with a student's sense of being treated fairly by the teacher.

In the Grade 11 business math class I taught I had a student who wouldn't work, as he got sidetracked too easily (quite often a problem in that class). In one class I had given them two assignments to be handed in. I had explained to them that full solutions were needed for full credit. This student was talking and I approached him in an indirect manner, not addressing his talking but focusing on the state of his assignment. I asked him if his assignment was completed and ready to hand in. He replied it was, so I asked him if he had shown full solutions and he said, 'No.' (I later found out he was unaware of the requirements). I gave him the choice to finish the work or hand it in incomplete and move on to the next assignment. He said he wasn't going to do the extra work involved in doing full solutions. He was adamant, and was becoming quite loud so my associate took the opportunity to step in. Eventually my associate and I convinced him to complete the work. After talking to this student, I found out that he did not feel he was being treated fairly. I think that is the key to why he refused to work. Once he cooled down and felt he was being treated fairly, he was not a problem and did not resist.

* * * * *

Learning to teach involves learning the delicate relationship between management problems and how one teaches. Quite simply, changing one's approach and thinking it through carefully can often produce a significant improvement, simply because the teacher is working harder to 'tune in' to students' responses and to include engaging activities.

I think a significant event occurred when I was giving the students notes. I moved to writing on the blackboard at the suggestion of my associate. I agreed because of the intensity of the rebuke I felt from the students when I used the overhead. I went home that afternoon and reviewed the day with a mind to better my presentation. I decided that I needed to learn to write on and use the chalkboard to give essential notes to students. I also decided to vary my presentation, punctuate the lesson with practical applications of the theory or information. I concluded that an entire lesson could not be successful without getting the students involved or taking active participation in the lesson.

When I met with the class on the second day, I gave them a worksheet. The students were encouraged to discuss the questions, and use their textbooks and me as a resource to complete the worksheet. Everyone, myself included, appeared to have a more positive experience in class on the second day. The next time I plan a lesson I will attempt to provide at least two activities (i.e., a short note and another activity). I will plan the lesson in such a way that a break for discussion or a question and answer period will be a part of it.

* * * * *

One of the new teacher's many challenges involves the amount of structure required to engage students successfully in revision and preparation for a test. This short passage shows again the close relationship between engaging students in productive activities and reducing the need for 'management' of a group's behaviour.

I gave my Grade 9 class the period before a test to work on several practice problems I had put on the board. I told them the questions were not due for homework but only for study purposes, in preparation for the test. I quickly realized that 70 minutes of test preparation time with no questions assigned, but only 'suggested', turned into 70 minutes of talking with your friends about nothing related to science!

The next time I taught the class before a major unit test I drastically changed my preparation format. I made up a mock test for the students to work on for the period, making sure it was challenging and covered the material on the test. Because it was only a mock test I allowed the students to do the test open book. For the last half-hour of the class, I took up questions students had problems with on the mock test. I found the second time went much more smoothly than the first. The students were forced to remain concentrated on studying for the entire period.

* * * * *

Every school has its own way of responding when a student is 'sent to the office'. In this instance, the unexpected result was interpreted by the new teacher as a message that this was not a useful way to deal with a difficult student.

Only once did I send a student to the office and I will not soon do it again. A certain student was being very disruptive in class. After many attempts to settle him down, I decided that the only way for the class to have a little peace was to banish him. I called down to the office and sent the student away. About 5 minutes after I had sent him to the office they shipped him back with a little note which I was to fill out with the reason I was giving him a detention. The reason I dismissed him was to remove him from the class, not necessarily to give him a detention.

* * * * *

New teachers often create interesting strategies for 'changing the pace' to keep a lesson going. Here one individual offers a very specific management strategy for a lesson involving extensive questioning by the teacher.

I like asking questions of students who aren't listening, as a form of discipline. A good break in the class is to have everybody stand up and walk once around the room and return to their seat but not sit down. Comment that those who sat down aren't listening. Then have everyone standing and ask the class quick questions. When a student answers correctly, he or she sits. Those sitting down can still be asked questions. Stop the game when two or three students are left standing to prevent massive depression for a single last person.

* * * * *

Just as too little direction can generate confusion and disorder, too much direction in the form of too many new terms can also generate problems. 'Reading' when students are frustrated can be just as important as recognizing when they are bored.

> My first day of teaching was my most significant. I drastically overestimated the ability of the class. Not their scholastic ability, mind you, but their working ability. The first unit I taught was curve sketching which has a lot of information which must be introduced before the actual sketching can begin. With this in mind, I decided to do a review note on derivatives, and another on what different values for the derivatives meant; I introduced new terms like cusp, concavity, increasing vs. decreasing slopes, increasing and decreasing functions and asymptotes. This added up to $1\frac{1}{2}$ pages of notes (words, not numbers) with no examples yet included. This was unheard of in math classes.
>
> In the next class, I included diagrams and large examples among the notes, an approach that was widely accepted as an improvement. I did this since the class was struggling and seemed frustrated, so I did not want to turn them off math any more than they already were. Ironically, I was able to get them to write more notes with this method than with what I did originally. Next time, I'll start with this method.

* * * * *

This longer passage reveals the importance of precise instructions to a group of 14-year-olds. The author also demonstrates the benefit that accrues to the teacher who watches students' responses closely and attempts thoughtful changes in the next lesson.

> I learned a lot about teaching high school during my last teaching work term. In my first week of teaching, I was still in university mode after just finishing the summer semester. This quickly changed after I realized that high school is not the place to be giving a lecture.
>
> In early September, I was giving a lesson on the metric system. The night before I had gone over my lesson plan to make sure that I was ready for this day. I was teaching a Grade 9 science class with a wide range of abilities in the class. I found that I had to give them exact instructions about what they were supposed to do.
>
> During the lesson already mentioned, I was not very specific as to whether they were to have their books open or closed. Some of the brighter students had their books open, trying to take notes about what I was saying and most of the other students had not bothered to open their books. I gave my lesson orally to the class. I had prepared

several good examples which I proceeded to put onto the board with little detail. This prompted the rest of the class to go leafing through their books to find a piece of paper to copy my examples. The lesson was disrupted, and I had to wait until they settled down again.

My initial plan had been to give my lesson, followed by the examples, while the students had their books closed and were paying attention only to me. Now I realize that they figured that I would erase the board and the information would never be seen again. This was not my intention at all. I wrote up a very simple note that they would be given ample time to copy into their notebooks. I provided the examples with detail as how to approach the problem and how to answer the problem.

The next day I taught the same class of Grade 9 science students. I changed my plan of attack for this day. I did not get any complaints from the students about the previous day but I noticed how much more smoothly things went when I gave precise instructions. On the second day, I gave them a review of the metric lesson. I asked them to keep their books closed and answer the questions by raising their hand as I asked them. My lesson for this day was on area. I told them to keep their books closed during my discussion and a note would be provided on the board afterwards along with relevant examples. They were assured that they would have enough time to copy the information. During this lesson, I wrote key words on the board which gave them something to focus on while I was talking. My lesson went faster the second day, too, because the students were very attentive.

I picked up many small points that will help me with my teaching in the future. I learned a great deal in my first few weeks of teaching. In high school, and especially Grade 9, the students are not as independent as they are in university. High school students need guidance and the teacher's job is to provide that for them. After that incident, I made sure that my instructions were perfectly clear and everyone knew what they were supposed to do.

* * * * *

Another longer passage that focuses on the relationship between homework, quizzes and tests concludes with a reminder that those learning to teach should not set themselves the high standard of 'getting it right' the first time. Only experience can teach the lessons expressed here. And until one masters these lessons, management problems are likely to occur more frequently.

The situation I describe here concerns my Grade 12 physics class, and I begin with some background information. Until this point, I had been assigning homework almost every night but I only collected it periodically. I had assigned review questions on the Monday before the test (the test was on Friday). I took the test questions directly from the review questions (though I changed the wording slightly). I marked the tests over the weekend and I was very surprised to find that the class average was only 65. I had assumed that since the questions were from the homework and they had had plenty of time for extra help they would all do very well.

The next day I returned their tests and went over the solutions. For each test question I gave them the page and question number for the corresponding review question. I explained to the class where I got the test questions from and that I wasn't sure why three of them had marks below 50 per cent. At that point I had figured out that although I was assigning homework every night they obviously were not completing that homework.

That day we all started following a new homework policy. Their homework would be collected every day and it would be marked for completeness and correct answers. Each night's homework would be given a mark out of 10. In order to determine how effective my new homework plan was I took the questions for the second test out of the homework again. The class average was 4 per cent higher. I think that collecting and marking the homework gave them incentive to have it finished, and by completing their homework they got more practice answering the types of questions that would be on the tests.

Most of the students in my class were very close friends, and I was a little concerned that they would just copy homework questions from each other so I implemented another idea. Each day I gave a 10–15 minute quiz on the same type of question that was done for home-work the night before. Although I didn't have time to do this absolutely every day it was very effective. The students knew that they should expect a quiz so they made sure that they knew how to do the home-work questions. I think that my ideas worked well, and next time I will know to start these things at the beginning of the school year rather than waiting until after the first test. One change that I would make to the quiz idea is that, rather than giving them a quiz Tuesday on Monday night's homework, I will give them a quiz Wednesday on Monday night's homework. This gives those who had trouble with the homework a day to get help.

* * * * *

Many new teachers experience the problem of classroom 'chatter' that seems harmless at first and then rises to intolerable levels. The author of this passage reveals a clever way of explaining why assigned seats were being changed and concludes with plans for 'next time'.

The students I worked with had been allowed by my supervisor to choose their own seats. Those who knew each other clustered together in groups of three or four and I had one student who decided to sit alone. At first the chatter was at a comfortable, acceptable level. Things quickly changed as the days went by.

On one occasion, a particularly loud student mocked another student outside her circle of friends during group discussion. I believe the only reason she acted out was because she wanted to impress her 'clique' and audience. I spoke with the student afterwards and decided the entire class needed a change of perspective. I implemented a new seating plan the next day. I was swamped with groans, grumbles, and mumbles when I told them at the beginning of the next class that I was going to move everyone around. I didn't tell them it was to split up the talkers, I told them it was so they might experience the class from a different perspective in the room and meet different people. They bought it, and it worked!!!

I was also able to move easily distracted students away from traffic areas like seats beside windows, doors, and the back of the room. They paid more attention to the lessons without the tempting outside stimuli. I tried to put kids together who could work well collectively and not reject one another on the basis of her popularity (or lack thereof). The groups became more productive and, since the members didn't have too much in common, the groups had nothing better to do but work on the task at hand.

Next time, I would like to put students in alphabetical order right from day one. I think that this often splits up the threesomes and foursomes in the class and scatters them around the room. However, I would tell them that the alphabetical order makes it easier for me to learn their names and take attendance. In a month's time, once the students become accustomed to the rules and routines of the classroom, I would let them switch seats and make up their own seating plan. I would stress the importance of avoiding distractions and the benefits of sitting beside someone who could help her with her work or who she might help. I would give them the opportunities to move again at the start of each month.

* * * * *

While every teacher faces the extra demands of taking a class on a field trip, science teachers face the challenge of managing a large group during practical activities. With 14-year-olds, as in this passage, one experience of 'chaos' is usually all that is required to prompt a new statement of expectations. Here again we hear that discussing a frustrating event with experienced teachers plays a useful role in deciding just how to recover and move forward.

It was only the second full class I had taught to these students. My supervising teacher, who was normally there, was away, so a supply teacher was to sit in and observe me. However, the supply teacher was not there much so, in essence, *I was the supply teacher.* Ahhhh!!!!

Class started out all right. I collected a lab [their formal reports of an experimental activity] they had done a few classes earlier. Next I had them pull out a lab that they had prepared the previous class to be done today. The students in charge of textbooks got the books for their row. I know this wasn't the best order to do these things in, and next time I would have them get the books out first, but it turned out all right and they got done what they had to, and speedily settled in.

We quickly reviewed safety in the lab and started working on the lab. The lab involved describing physical properties of various substances. To minimize movement and avoid confusion, the students passed each substance to the person behind them every few minutes. The last person in the row brought it to the front of the next row and so forth. This was done in contrast to having the students move from station to station. I would definitely do this the same way next time; it worked well.

Once the lab was completed, the problems began. We had emphasized the importance of washing hands after handling chemicals, but being in a new lab I could only find one bottle of soap. To keep the water flying around to a minimum I had the kids form a line at the front sink. Some got a few drops of water splashed on them, but nothing terrible. Then, paper towels, where were they? I finally found one roll. In the midst of the hand-washing/hand-drying confusion I realized I had forgotten to tell them about the discussion questions they had to report on, and the lab had to be handed in at the end of class. I tried to tell them, but of course not one listened (well, maybe one or two). Finally I got them settled and told them, but they were so wound up very few actually got to work and did the questions. I realize this was partly my fault and I would definitely remember next time to be sure I told them everything BEFORE they got up and moved around. I talked the discouraging class over with my colleagues, and they said the class didn't sound so terrible to them. With some ideas and encouragement from them I was ready for them next day.

First I told the students just how disappointed I was with their behaviour the day before. I made it clear that if I was talking, or if someone in the class was asking a question, they all had to respect that person. That meant they had to stop, be quiet, and listen — it might be important. Class went great from here. Once I made my expectations clear, and made them realize I wouldn't stand for any nonsense, their test of me was over and they were as good as any Grade 9 class can be.

* * * * *

Knowing how to prepare and knowing when one is adequately prepared are two of the new teacher's many challenges, particularly on the first day with a class. While some teachers wish students would ask more questions, this final passage on management shows how students can 'turn the tables' on a teacher who realizes in mid-lesson that his or her preparation is inadequate. The lessons we learn on our first day are often among our most memorable.

> I did not prepare for this class as much as I should have. I knew the material in the textbook, and felt I could therefore teach the information and answer any pertinent questions. I was wrong, and got smoked. The class decided they were going to be intellectual, and wanted to know all the specifics. I found myself trying to balance equations, figure out oxidation numbers, and explain why this compound reacted this way when in water, and why this compound was insoluble etc. I had decided to use the blackboard for this lesson, and had planned out in my lesson plan how it would appear to the students. By the time the lesson was over and I walked to the back of the class to admire my handiwork, I started to laugh. It didn't even look close to what I had intended. I could barely follow my own thought process. I immediately walked back to my workroom, sat at my desk and worked out every equation. I researched all the chemicals involved, so I could try to explain all their 'Why?' questions. I went well beyond what was covered in the textbook in hopes that I could find more than one approach to explaining this topic. I made up overheads to help with the explanations. I then went back to the classroom and taught the class again to the empty room.
>
> A much more confident and prepared teacher walked into the class the next day. I knew there would be questions, and I had prepared for them. I knew I would need more than one approach to teaching this topic, and I had them. I used the blackboard efficiently, I used the overhead, I even had a video on standby (just in case). The point is, I was prepared. I took time to examine what I was teaching and tried to anticipate. I knew more than I had to — and that was good, I needed to. It was a wonderful class. You could tell I had reached the students. Questions asked of me were answered with confidence. Questions asked of the students were answered with insight and understanding. I learned a hard and embarrassing lesson the first day, and would try to never let it happen again.

Reading these testimonials raises the question, 'What makes the difference between pre-service teachers and more experienced teachers?' Does the classroom management fairy pay a visit to those about to start their second year of teaching? After their first year, are teachers abducted by aliens, only to return with some strange form of extrasensory perception? The difference must be the experience itself. I am sure that in every pre-service teacher education program there is a place for classroom management. But is it enough that someone tells you to 'establish clear classroom procedures from the outset'? Is it enough that someone tells you to 'be prepared for classes in advance'? Is it enough that someone tells you to 'vary your teaching approach from day to day'? If it were enough, would we need experience before being given classes of our own?

'Just because you teach your class something doesn't mean they'll learn it.' The same probably holds true for pre-service teacher education. Just because you've been told that you will need to establish procedures for ensuring that students are doing their homework regularly doesn't mean that you'll learn to do that. I can honestly say from my own early teaching that my problems with classroom management were so 'spur of the moment' that I forgot anything that I 'should' have done, and I did what I thought (and hoped) was right — if I had any time to think at all. Afterwards, I thought about it, discussed things with other teachers, vice-principals, and principals — you name it — and tried to decide how I had done, and how I might do it differently (and better!) next time. Sometimes I initiated these discussions, and sometimes my associate did. Regardless of who spoke first, the point is that I don't think that I had really learned anything until I had lived it. Only after I had lived it did things start to make sense. Furthermore, it made sense to me during my courses at the Faculty of Education, when other colleagues — including both pre-service teachers and professors — told me something about their own personal experiences of teaching. I think the main reason was that we were engaged in conversation about what we had experienced, and each of us was trying to make sense of the other's point of view as it related to our own.

Thus the difference between an experienced teacher and a pre-service teacher in the area of classroom management lies in the experience. When one encounters more situations in the classroom, more pieces of the puzzle fall into place. As one continues to learn as a teacher, it becomes increasingly easy to develop strategies and approaches to make the pieces fit.

Drawing The Line

Both pre-service teachers and experienced teachers are in positions requiring them to maintain a certain professional distance from their pupils. There is no right answer to exactly where The Line is drawn in a relationship between being the pupils' friend and being their teacher. This problem is further compounded for the pre-service teacher, who is often the youngest teacher in the school. In the case of secondary school teachers, a pre-service teacher may have been away from secondary school for only four or five years. The writing that follows suggests that this is an important issue in teacher development.

The last three weeks were, as predicted, very learning-intense for me. I learned a great deal, met some great kids, got a little glimpse of what they were capable of, and discovered some of the other inherent aspects of their lives that existed beyond the little classroom window that I saw.

I think my greatest problem over the three weeks was the limitation of my own creativity. Coming up with demos and labs, interesting stories (!!!), good answers to the students' infrequent questions, and basically entertaining was the toughest part for me. The entertainer in me was stressed occasionally by the perception that my audience was bored. Having been a member of a few audiences helped affirm that.

This brings me to one of my favourite theories about problems applying to specific people. I find something missing when we talk about how to get classes to pay attention, how we deal with problem students, etc., etc. While I can appreciate that examples of previous solutions are good things to be aware of, they can never replace the real thing or the actual problem. Every problem has at least one aspect which is unique to it, that being the student himself. 'Hypothetical' is fun, but for me, I like to approach the problem before it is one and get to know the student. When I say 'get to know the student', I don't mean name, average, family occupations and two aspects of his personal life, but actually get to know him; how he approaches problems in general, what motivates him in everyday life, what his views are that affect how he perceives things in the world around him, and how he reacts to outside influences or pressures, or authorities. Once you know this much, most problems can be, if not necessarily preempted, at least dealt with quickly.

I began to feel on the last day like part of the school. Seeing students outside the class and talking to them without the classroom atmosphere was wonderful. I started to pursue my own little interests and not just hang out with the four people I knew. This was a good feeling, which made me wish I could stay. These last three weeks have been physically and emotionally draining. I think I flirted with that little line between teacher and peer a few times but, seeing that it was my first attempt, I think I am quite comfortable with being able to distinguish it, and convey that distinction to the students as well.

* * * * *

The following account illustrates vividly the complexities of establishing relationships with individual students. It is one thing to discover that a student is behind in his progress because of time spent in jail, and it is quite another to discover that claiming to have spent time in jail is being used as a 'cover' for an even more complex problem. Finding the balance in personal relationships is challenging for students as well as for teachers.

While I was a teacher's aide for a Grade 10 general math class, I got pretty close to a lot of my students. Many of these students came from broken homes or were involved with gangs, but all in all they were really good kids. I developed an especially close relationship with one student, who can be known here as 'Bill.' Bill wasn't too keen on math, but he did grasp the concepts pretty quickly when he tried. He seemed like a typical kid. Anyway, my point is that I really cared about Bill. One day, he told me that he was a year behind but it wasn't because he was stupid. It was because he had missed a term of school earlier. When I asked him why, he replied that he had been arrested, and had to spend some time in jail for beating up another student. The jail sentence wasn't very long, but he had to transfer schools, so he ended up missing one term. I figured this was no big deal. He was here now and he was doing well. I only helped out with this class three times a week, and one week I noticed that Bill wasn't around. I assumed this was because he was sick. Then I found out from my associate that he was having personal problems, and wouldn't be back for a while. I felt I should leave it at that, so I did. Finally, when it was getting near the end of term, I asked my associate about him again. She told me that Bill had been in the hospital for over thirty days because he was diagnosed as being manic-depressive. I couldn't believe it. I don't know if I was more upset because it was so unfair, or because I hadn't asked sooner.

I had been so concerned with that line between personal versus professional that I really felt as if I had done something wrong. I ended up finding out which hospital he was in, went to visit him, and discovered he had been released earlier that day. It was really awful — almost like a very bad movie — but it was real life. To top it off, I found out that this had happened to him before, and that was why he was already one term behind. Bill had never been arrested; that's just what he told people. I was really shaken by the whole situation. I tried to act like it was no big deal, but it was. I still think it was so unfair. Bill didn't really like school too much as it was, and now he was even further behind. I still worry about whether he's going to finish school or not. I really hope so. I did end up calling his home before I left for Kingston, and we talked for a while. He told me what had happened, and we exchanged numbers. I told him to call me if he ever needed anything, but I didn't really think he would. He really appreciated the call and the concern. I think it meant a lot to him and that made me feel a little better, but I still think it really sucks. I guess if there's anything that I learned from all of this, it was that it's really okay to care about your students, not to assume that you know what goes on in their lives outside of the classroom, and most importantly, not to worry about what you should or shouldn't do. There are no cut-and-dried rules about how personal you are allowed to be, so do what feels right, and don't worry about the rest.

It's Not Really My Class, Is It?

Teacher candidates often wrestle with the fact that they are not teaching their own classes. For both legal and professional reasons, in most contexts the teacher-in-training is working with an associate teacher. There are varying degrees of control of the class that the associate will permit, based on an assessment of what the class and the beginning teacher seem ready for. Even if the associate teacher gives you lots of space to 'do your own thing,' there are times when you realize that you just are not the one in control of what happens in what might feel like your classroom. If you factor the students in on top of that, then it can be quite troubling. Students do not always take well to pre-service teachers in their classroom, where they are used to being taught by someone else. While not every new teacher may experience this tension, those who do, find it quite memorable and significant.

> I taught one unit in the same way as my associate would have, with massive overhead assault. After completion of this unit I said, 'Wait a minute, I really don't like that!!' And I decided to say, 'I don't care how he teaches, I don't teach this way.' The next unit was totally different. These kids are OAC [Ontario Academic Credits — university-entrance courses for 18-year-olds], they can make their own notes. I focused all of my energy into teaching, and not overhead preparation. There were some groans when I told them to make their own notes, but the response to good solid teaching at the blackboard was great. They seemed to really like that better. After that, I only once made overheads for them all year. In fact, even my supervisor began to alter his style.

* * * * *

There were times when I did not feel so good being a teacher. For example, on occasion I had to be put into a disciplinary role, and when the students messed up I felt badly that I had to discipline them. Sometimes they wouldn't listen to me, and I felt even worse! It meant that I would have to reprimand them even further and, because I had been disobeyed, I took it personally that they did not respect my authority. That was the worst, *when I felt that I did not have the respect of the students.*

Mind you, not all of the students were like that. Some were very nice and they made the whole thing worthwhile. It was these people, who showed that they respected that I was there to be a teacher, and a friend, who made me want to go back and have the opportunity to be able to teach in front of the class again. Plus, I want to be able to correct all the mistakes that I made in the first round.

* * * * *

In a short teaching placement, a beginning teacher is always aware that another individual with much more experience is the 'owner' of the class. In a longer teaching placement that begins on the first day of the school year, the issue of ownership is more complex. In the following account, the teacher candidate comes to terms with a decision taken by 'Jeff', who is the associate teacher and real 'owner' of the class.

This is the very first time that I have had this feeling — the feeling of teaching someone else's class. Until this point in the course, I had pretty much been able to do what I wanted, and had been having a great time with the students. Suddenly I am not able to do one thing that I want to, and I feel horrible! It is only one thing, but to me it is important. And we discussed it, and it doesn't look like he will accept anything that I have to say about this issue. Am I feeling imprisoned? No matter what descriptor I use, it still comes out the same way.

I think this may be something that is a problem with teacher education. Certainly my case is not isolated — there must be others who feel the same. In fact, I would guess that there are a lot of them . . . This gets back to the whole issue of supervision in teaching placements, and the issue of evaluation, and the artificiality of practice teaching situations. In one sense, I thought that the fact that I was in this program with extended 16-week teaching placements would make me sort of 'immune' to this type of feeling/treatment. Apparently not. The fact of the matter is that although I am teaching for four months, *it is still artificial.* It is not my own class, and therefore I cannot always do what I want. I am forced to look at it this way — I do not see this difference of opinion/style as a source of conflict between Jeff and me. I think that both Jeff and I are mature enough to handle the situation, and it will not cause any problems in terms of evaluation of my teaching. More importantly, I see the disagreement as a source of conflict between the students and myself — and to me that is the most important relationship, and it had the potential to put that relationship in jeopardy.

* * * * *

The next voice to be heard ranges over a number of issues, beginning with the issue of ownership and the associated issue of authority. The author speaks to the issue of 'critical friends' in reference to the fact that two individuals were assigned to the same three-week placement during their studies at Queen's, so that they could observe and offer comments to each other. Finally, the author turns to the perennial topic of 'good grades', 'good students', and 'intelligence'.

During my practicum it was easy to get along with one class and easy to get frustrated with another class. I think the Grade 10s saw me more as a substitute teacher. They thought I didn't really have any authority and they weren't going to learn anything from me. They figured out that I was going to teach them, but I don't think I got much respect as an authority figure. That goes back to ownership of the class. I only taught these students for two weeks and I didn't feel as though I had ownership. The students probably sensed this. I went into the Grade 12 class expecting to become friends with them. I think they sensed that.

I tried things I probably wouldn't have before. I tried new things I wouldn't have thought about trying before taking education courses, like kids pushing each other around on carts to learn relative velocities. I made a serious effort to organize the notes I put on the board. And I reflected on my lessons a lot more.

Critical friends: I see pros and cons of this. Some cons first. Everybody has a different teaching style and different perspectives on what kids are asking or need to know to understand better. When I watched my critical friend, he did a great job. However, even though he was doing a good job I would think stuff like this: 'I would have said . . .', 'The kid wants to know . . .', 'Do this demo now or use this as an example . . .' The things I picked out for improvement my critical friend already knew. I guess the bottom line as I see it is that the critical friend is beneficial, but we'd benefit more from actually teaching another class.

I've been calling 'good' students the ones who get good grades — normally. By my own definition 'good students' also referred to my hyper, rowdy kids who scored well on my test. Our society pigeonholes kids into 'good' or 'smart', depending on what number they get on a given test in a given subject at a given time. What I would like to do when I teach is try to change that point of view a little. Let kids know that our whole society seems to be based on the performance on tests in school, when geniuses could be coming through our school system who don't score well on tests. Society won't change overnight, so kids should still try to excel on tests, but realize with more open minds that 'smart' and 'good' students really means that they did well on some tests and, since they did, society sees them as intelligent. Really, they could be trained pieces of wood. (Do I sense an analogy coming on?) We can teach dogs to do tricks, seals to do tricks, whales to do tricks, even mice. Can we train people to do well on tests, then mistake the regurgitated action or reaction as intelligence? Another question: How can I, as a teacher, modify my classes and tests so that more of the 'untrained' and 'natural' intelligence appears on the test? As a teacher, will I become a 'trainer' and, by so doing, will I be able to create such a test (a test that tests natural intelligence not regurgitation)? I'm kind of scared how 'deep' this got.

To close this section of the book, we include a letter sent to Derek Featherstone by a beginning teacher who, during his orientation, had received an early draft of some of the materials in this collection. Like the other contributions to this section, the letter is filled with emotions and thoughts common to many beginning teachers.

Hi Derek,

I am one of the student teachers out on my first teaching term from September to December. I am writing because of your book, and I want to tell you how it has had a direct impact on me as a pre-service teacher.

I have been a student teacher at this high school for the past couple of weeks, and it has been an amazing and rewarding experience, with the possible exception of today. I was recruited by the science department head to help coach the Junior Boys' Volleyball team. What she didn't tell me was that the word 'help' was for the purposes of administration, and that really the team was mine. I love coaching, and as a team, we are working very hard, and having a great time! What I didn't plan for, nor realize, was the amount of energy and time that go into coaching. When I think back to high school, I can't remember my coaches looking as tired as I feel after the end of a practice or game. Anyway, we had a game Thursday night, and I came home at 7:00 after an extremely long day to a pile of marking that I had promised my Grade 11 Biology class that I would have marked for the next day. I was up till quarter to one in the morning doing my marking, and then was at school this morning at 8:30, tired, exhausted, but feeling on top and in control.

I guess the problems started in the staff room. Several older teachers were sitting around complaining about their students, and trying to decide who had the worst students! I have never heard more pessimism, or cynicism in my life! What made things worse, was that these very teachers were the ones who arrived fifteen minutes before school, and left as soon as it was over. I felt like going up to them and asking them what the heck they thought teaching was all about! When I returned from lunch, they kept on complaining about every subject under the sun. From pay freezes, and Professional Development, to criticizing the administration and the board.

Over the past couple of days, I had noticed that my two associates never ate their lunch in the staff room, and during our third period I mentioned how I refused to eat lunch in the staff room again. My associate immediately knew how I felt! He avoided the staff room for the same reason, and he proceeded to tell me some things about teaching. We talked about everything from the 75% average the administration expects from OAC class, to the rift between older and younger staff over pay and seniority. We discussed the effect of destreaming on schools. We talked about the hours that you have to put in to be on top of your work as a teacher, and how parents reacted to poor grades. I guess I had been a little naive as to the politics involved with being a teacher. I had assumed that teachers were there because they wanted to be, and not just because it was a job.

I was a little disheartened and tired when I walked into my fourth period class, but things started to pick up when I was greeted with smiling faces, and eager questions from the night's homework. I have found that, if there is a single 'grade' to teach, then for me it is definitely Grade 11. They are so eager to learn and full of questions that it is all I can do to even follow a lesson plan! Unfortunately, my associate had saved a difficult concept for me to teach on a Friday afternoon in the last period of the day. Try explaining and demonstrating electron affinity, ionization energy, atomic radius, and all of the trends on a Friday, with a school football game going on outside. Let's just say that it was a very difficult class, and I came home totally drained, and feeling somewhat isolated and alone with my thoughts and emotions.

The first thing I did was go straight for a nap. I woke up a few hours later, but I didn't feel refreshed. In fact I started to brood a little about the day. After supper, I returned to my room and pulled out the draft copy of your book. Talk about a positive experience! A lot of how I was feeling and some of the problems that I was facing were contained within the pages of your book. I spent two hours reading, and already I feel less alone, and better off than when I began. *It's great to know that others are experiencing the same things as I am, and that they sometimes feel the same way!*

I had my pen out as I went along, and I started underlining thoughts that were important to me. When I am finished, I will summarize my thoughts, and get them to you as soon as I can. I just wanted you to know that your book has the ability to become a positive influence on beginning teachers everywhere, and if you ever need any help with suggestions or material, please just ask! I am off to work on my next unit, and to try and think of a way to salvage my lesson on electron affinity, ionization energy and atomic radius. Who knows? Maybe I can get it right on Monday!

Yours in teaching and learning,
Colin Muscat

The Voice of a Poet Learning to Teach, 1

Tanya Marwitz

Spinning: Reflections on 'Learning to Fly' in a 'Pilot Program'

stomach spinning
heart racing
thoughts
thoughts
questions
concerns

why am I here again?
why the fresh start? new location? new peers?

my expectations: high
yours: unknown, unclear, undefined
until now

now, there's a light, a direction,
a compass pointing straight ahead
just go, Tanya
get into it
do, feel, experience

but always the questions
concerns

energy battles exhaustion as hope overcomes fear
'each one teach one' is what she said
that's what I'll do and I'll start with one:
ME.

Every hour has that 'new car' smell
the change is exhilarating — and draining — and valuable

so many questions as I walk through a door
whose size, shape, weight and resistance I'm unsure of

will I catch my foot walking through?
will it swing in both directions or
will it slam shut behind me?
will it lead to new doors . . . ?

still spinning
still wondering
still hoping . . .

(August 1996, just before my four-month placement)

Chapter 3

The Personal Nature of Teaching and Learning Experiences

Introduction by Derek Featherstone

As teachers we often hear the saying, 'If I can help just one person's life to be better, then what I am doing is worth it.' When I received the letter that appears at the end of Chapter 2, I found it rewarding to know that the initial draft of this collection had helped a beginning teacher in some way. Then, as I re-read the letter, I thought that there was something more to it than validation for the work that had been put into the book. I read more about this beginning teacher's experience in the staffroom. This was not simply an experience. It was an experience where the teacher was also a learner. This teacher has now created his own view of schools and how things work, based not only on personal experience, but also on an interpretation of that experience.

There is growing interest in the role of experience in learning. In particular, there is a growing body of educational research that looks at the role of experience in the process of learning to teach. Several recent publications include pre-service teachers writing about their experiences (Knowles, Cole, and Presswood, 1994; Bullough, Knowles, and Crow, 1991), and we see this collection as an important addition to that material. We have tried to make this book unique by giving emphasis to the pre-service teachers' own words as they develop a sense of professional voice. We are focusing on their personal reflections, their insights and their commentaries on experiences of learning to teach. While comments and assistance from professors can be of tremendous value in learning to teach, they do not directly foster *the development of voice* that we believe is central to continuing to learn from experience in the earliest years of teaching, when career-long patterns and habits may be established. Here our emphasis is on a community of pre-service teachers, working collaboratively to share and make sense of their experiences learning to teach.

In April 1994, a class of pre-service teachers completed their education courses at Queen's University. One celebration of their collaboration that term involved producing a book chronicling their own development as teachers, not only through their education courses, but also over the preceding four months when they all taught in various settings under the guidance of associate teachers. In 1995, another class in the same program produced a similar book that was equally exciting and personal in nature. These two books form the foundation of several chapters in this collection. In the two books, the beginning teachers examine their experiences with a view to identifying and interpreting the learning that is *in* their teaching experiences. The introduction to the 1994 book describes the initial spirit behind the collection of material in *Finding a Voice While Learning to Teach*.

Why We Are Doing This ...

The original thrust for this document was based upon the fact that we are unique from most other education students in that we have all experienced four months of classroom teaching before arriving at Queen's. A forum for discussion of the situations and issues we encountered seemed necessary in order to allow us to concentrate on these issues and to let our individual and collective voices to be heard.

By meeting once a week on a specific topic or issue, we hope to compile a valuable resource from which we can identify problem situations and have a record as to how some of our colleagues handled each situation. This reference should allow us to pull pieces out of each others' style and decide what is comfortable for us as individuals. When reading this book, it is important to remember that the things included herein are not the only ways of doing things. They are merely suggestions and recollections of our experiences. Using this information from our peers and the information from our other courses, each of us has the opportunity to begin to formulate our own philosophies of education — something we all need to keep in mind as educators and lifelong learners.

We hope this proves to be a worthwhile resource throughout our careers in education, helping us to survive not only in the first few years of teaching but also in later years when we can really start to become ourselves ...

This introduction echoes three issues with implications for learning to teach and teacher education:

1　It recognizes the inevitable concerns that beginning teachers have with classroom management and finding one's place within a school as a beginning teacher.
2　It recognizes the personal nature of teaching and learning.
3　Above all, it recognizes that while others cannot tell you exactly what to do in every situation, they can help you to think about your own successes and setbacks to help you learn more about teaching and learning.

Over the years we have all heard statements to the effect that each of us learns differently — that some are 'hands-on' learners, some are visual learners, some are auditory learners, and so on. The same holds true for those of us learning to teach. Each of us learns to teach differently and, subsequently, each of us will teach differently. Likewise, we all have our own reasons for doing the things that we do in the classroom. We base them on those ideals we value in terms of what we think education should and could be. This section ends with responses from a section of the 1995 group's book to the question, 'What does it all mean?' They have worked hard to answer this question in their own minds during their education courses and teaching placements. To me, these words are testimony to the personal nature of teaching and learning as they show tremendous variety in terms of the issues that are at the forefront of their minds. They serve as a reminder to me that, just as this group of pre-service teachers shows such incredible variation, so too will all the groups of students that any of us ever teach. I hope that the words describing 'What does it all mean?' serve as catalysts for others learning to teach, as they reflect on this very question and on their own teaching and learning experiences.

A Good Teacher Focuses on Students

I think that if you look at yourself and realize that your focus in the classroom is curriculum, you're missing something. I've struggled with the feeling of insecurity because I was afraid that my students might realize that I didn't know it all. My focus was wrong. Knowing the curriculum does not make a good teacher (although I believe it makes the job easier). From what I can tell, a good teacher is someone who is focused on his/her students. When you teach this way, I think that you develop a more successful learning environment, and from there the curriculum will fall into place.

* * * * *

The Personal Nature of Teaching and Learning Experiences

Take Risks and Expect the Unexpected

What is teaching? We go out on a four-month practicum not knowing what teaching is. So, we take the plunge into that experience, risking everything we've learned from our past as a learner. It's like you never really know how it feels to canoe down a river that runs hard through the rapids until you have experienced it. What do you look for? My only advice is: when you least expect it, expect it! There will be many unexpected turns, but the deposits of quietness have allowed me to reflect. How do I make sense of everything? I believe our learning experiences at Queen's are not so immediate. During my three-week Queen's practicum, I learned that one of the toughest things to do was to know what the students don't understand. The heart of teaching is taking risks to get to places when you really don't know where you are going. These experiences will bridge the gaps between teaching and learning, even though I still don't know what it all really means.

* * * * *

Becoming a Better Teacher Does Not Happen Overnight

For me, it started with a desire to make the world a 'better' place to live: safer, healthier, and more educated. I also love working with children and adolescents, so teaching seemed to be an occupation that I would enjoy and which encompassed these three aspects.

I was initially leery about coming to McArthur as I didn't know many of my classmates before coming here and I thought it was a lot of money to fork out for one semester. However, now I'm glad I came and experienced this program. It gave me the opportunity to see many different styles of teaching, some that worked and some that didn't, so that I can incorporate what I liked and avoid what I didn't like from each into my own style. This isn't going to happen over-night; I'd be foolish to think it would since learning is a lifelong process, but it will develop and become 'refined' with practice. As well, and more importantly, I believe my time here has given me a chance to look at myself, my abilities and my weaknesses, and to work within my capabilities. This has built my self-esteem and my confidence. As a result, I feel I will make a better teacher, and the students, my main focus, will benefit from my growth. I look forward to our next opportunity to be in the classroom so I can put what I've learned into practice, and develop as a teacher.

* * * * *

Share Your Passion for Life and Learning

The past two terms have been filled with personal and professional development. My growth as a person has helped me become a better teacher, and my development as a teacher has made me a better person. My time at Queen's can be described as a lifestyle. It will be remembered for all the fun, friendships and learning that came with it. The bonds that have formed between some of us have reinforced the confidence that I have in others and also in myself. I have learned to live in the present — to take each day as it comes and to make the most of it because there will never be another like it. This passion for life and learning is something I want to share with my students. Most of all, I now realize that I will never have all the answers. Instead, I have learned to love the questions. If I don't have questions, then I'm not learning. And I hope I never stop learning because the only way to be a good teacher is to first be an active learner.

* * * * *

Learning to Teach Is an Amazing Process

What does it all mean? That's a tough one. Everything we've experienced during T1 [the first sixteen-week teaching term], Q1 [education courses at Queen's], and our three-week practicum has meant so much, it's hard to simplify it. I think what it all boils down to is the amazing process of learning to teach learning. T1 was a trial-by-fire teaching experience. We taught classes for sixteen weeks with no previous training and acquired a general feel for the role of teacher. Yet we did not understand this role. Q1 was a 'What does it all mean?' experience. Our time at Queen's pieced together and gave meaning to everything that we saw, learned, felt and didn't understand during T1. It also gave us plenty of new information, ideas, and insight to take away with us for our future teaching experiences. Our first opportunity occurred during our three-week practicum. This brief period allowed us the chance to apply our new understanding of teaching. It was a fantastic opportunity to try new techniques and ideas. Everything we did as teachers seemed to make more sense. But Q1 also meant much more than this. It also meant friends and fun. I spent four months with twenty-two of the most wonderful people. Our common interests and goals made us a team, one that I think is unbeatable. So what does it all mean? It means the greatest learning experience I've ever had.

* * * * *

The Personal Nature of Teaching and Learning Experiences

Teachers Are Not Magicians

Queen's has taught me to ask more questions, think of why things work and then practice what I've learned. When you teach students, you give a little bit of yourself to them. I found at Queen's I learned how to better myself, to live life to the fullest and to be happy.

Queen's has given me time to think about teaching. I don't just want to teach math and science. I want to teach students how to live together on this earth peacefully and to appreciate the environment. To face problems and work together as a team to help solve them, yet encourage each student to be himself/herself and to always try his/her very best. Yet, I must remind myself that teachers are not magicians. We cannot change anyone else — we can only listen patiently to what they say, answer all questions kindly and let them make their own decisions.

* * * * *

Teacher Education Has Opened My Eyes to Teaching

This type of question is not easily answered in one page. I feel the beauty of this program is that it doesn't have to mean anything at this stage of the game. All that I have at this particular moment are pieces of the puzzle. I do not know how they all fit together. I have two years to piece together what this all means. My term here at Queen's has opened my eyes to teaching in ways that I never thought were possible. I have had time to think about my teaching here. Teaching is not about imparting my knowledge upon the student. We must get the student to carry the ball for the majority of the time. If there is anything that I have learned here, it must be that I have a long road to travel before I become a respected teacher. When I say 'respected teacher,' I mean respected in my own view. Teaching is a personal thing. It is what you want it to be. Not what anyone else wants it to be. But we must also remember the students. After all, they are the ones that we must reach. Teaching is the great balance between personal growth and student growth.

* * * * *

Open Your Mind and Develop Your Point of View

I have not learned at McArthur as I have learned before. I have always just memorized the textbook, done a few assignments and then written a test. This will not work at McArthur. Any books on teaching only contain the authors' points of view about teaching. Anything that anybody tells you about teaching is only their point of view also. Your point of view is the important one. This does not mean that your point of view must be different than all others, it just means that you must have one of your very own.

At first I viewed McArthur as another 'hoop' that I had to jump through. Until I realized that it was a very special 'hoop' that you will never completely pass through, I did not get much from it. I was in my 'tell me how to teach' mode. I finally found the switch to put me in 'open mind' mode and now I am consciously looking for teaching techniques that work for me and for my students. They are flying by at near light speeds and I hardly notice them before the next one comes along. The only way that I am going to find my way of teaching is to get into a classroom and try different techniques with them. But what works with one class may not work with another so you have to be able to adapt.

* * * * *

You Must Never Stop Learning How to Teach

McArthur is a source of many new revelations, the most important of which is that as an educator you must never stop learning how to teach. Education is constantly evolving and so must the teacher. Education is not a stagnant pool of concepts but a fast flowing river of exploration, evolving ideas and insights. It carries within its waters the seeds of knowledge that seek to take hold and grow. The students as well as the teachers are forced to deal with the trials and tribulations that arise as this particular river runs its course. Learning to teach is an ongoing process and a lifelong commitment. New teachers must develop an appreciation for the responsibilities that are an integral part of the job. Classes and discussions here at McArthur are an essential part of teacher education as they serve to reinforce and expand the foundation upon which our teaching style is built. The classes may be forgotten but the ideology that is such an important part of teacher education is not. Teacher education at McArthur is so very important because in order to become good teachers, teachers must become students and learn how to learn. We were a lump of iron with a desire to become a sword. We survived our trial by fire. Now we are the sword and seek to be sharp.

* * * * *

Your Students Must Trust You

There are few absolutes in teaching so all I can tell you is what I see from where I am right now. To learn to teach is to learn about yourself. Teaching will test every part of you: your knowledge, organization, patience and imagination. But these things aren't enough. To truly help someone in their quest to become, you must open your mind to see things the way they do and, more importantly, you must possess the passion to bring those kids to see that they matter in the grand scheme of things. That they can be much more than they thought they could. That the world is still full of opportunity and wonder.

All the best techniques will be of no use if the students don't trust you to lead them beyond what they know. Sincerity and your genuine interest in students are your best teaching allies. Don't be afraid to give of yourself. It can be a rough ride sometimes, but you must hold on because just when you think you don't make a difference, you will. Everyone has something to teach another. Find it in yourself; find it in others; and above all, never stop looking. A wise man once said 'There are more things in heaven and earth than in all your imaginations.'

References

BULLOUGH, R.V., JR., KNOWLES, J.G. and CROW, N.A. (1991) *Emerging as a Teacher,* London, Routledge.

KNOWLES, J.G., COLE, A.L. and PRESSWOOD, C. (1994) *Through Preservice Teachers' Eyes: Exploring Field Experiences through Narrative and Inquiry,* New York, Merrill.

Chapter 4

Voices from Three Weeks of Teaching

Overview

Many people learning to teach are assigned for periods of two, three, or four weeks, and we are aware that much of the writing in this volume reflects teaching assignments that last longer. The length of time in a classroom does make a difference to the learning opportunities. We include the following voices to show the enthusiasm and insights developed in a three-week school placement that followed six weeks of classes in education courses. All of the contributors are members of Tom Russell's secondary-science methods class; for some it was their first teaching placement, while for others it was the last short placement before a four-month assignment. When they returned from teaching, Tom asked them to write at the end of the first class about their learning from experience and he also invited them to offer comments about his efforts in the first six weeks to help them prepare to learn from experience.

Several contributors refer to POE, which is in-class shorthand for 'Predict, Observe, Explain.' This teaching strategy is taken from the Project for Enhancing Effective Learning, developed at Monash University and the University of Melbourne in Australia. The strategy attempts to increase student interest and motivation and engage students' prior conceptions by asking them to predict what might happen before showing them what will happen (in science) or presenting what did happen (as in history, for example). Several contributors were teaching in mathematics and geography rather than science, and they were pleased to discover that POE 'transferred' out of science, where they met it, into their other teaching subject.

Learning from Experience

Each voice heard in this chapter is introduced by a heading that introduces a central theme.

Conquer Your Nervousness, Involve the Students to Earn Their Respect

This method [learning from experience] is really the only way to learn to teach. The first day in the classroom I observed and quickly learned names. On the second day there were work periods, so I went around and helped students on an individual basis. The third day I jumped right in, teaching all the classes. Wayne, my associate, was very supportive of me; however, he didn't want me to latch onto his type of teaching — he wanted me to find my own style. Getting up in front of the class was a very stressful experience the first time, but I found as I taught and became involved with the lesson that I forgot about my nervousness. As I was bombarded with so *many* new things and situations the whole three weeks, I learned a lot from it. At times it was overwhelming. Now that I'm back at Queen's and reflecting on my practicum, I have come up with some conclusions. I think I got a good solid footing about the basics of teaching. I have learned how important it is to involve the students and to get (earn) their respect. Now that I'm back here and thinking about all the different ways to teach, I realize that I didn't try very many new ways. I plan to think about new methods (i.e., to involve all the students in different ways). I'm looking forward to trying new methods in my next practicum and I'm also planning to do some research while I'm here. I'd like to set up some units where the students would be doing group work and individual work. Maybe have different stations in the class. I'd like to hand over some of the responsibility of learning to the students. I'd also like to learn more about tests. I met a biology teacher who gives the alternative of doing oral tests. So I've come back from my practicum with a clearer idea of teaching and some ideas and thoughts which I want to investigate further.

* * * * *

Asking My Students for Feedback Made All the Difference

I hit _____ Secondary School bursting at the seams with excitement and enthusiasm. Armed with theories and techniques learned in isolation from the 'trenches,' I wanted to jump headfirst into hands-on experimentation. How well were these new theories and experiences from McArthur going to help me?

It was an interesting three weeks. Confined to a classroom routine that could not be further from the one I hoped to employ, I had to set aside much of my experimenting ambition and revert back to the old 'chalk-and-talk' method, squeezing in little bits of the hands-on manipulatives, and POE technique where I could. While I did my best to offer the students a chance to uncover the properties of linear equations and the laws and conventions of trigonometry for themselves, I found I was often providing the answers to questions that had not yet been formed by the students (an outcome I was desperately trying to avoid this round).

I did manage to include some slightly modified POE aspects to a lesson or two, adding an experimental aspect to math usually reserved for the sciences. The predict-vote-test approach seemed to really drive home to the students the message I was trying to convey. I'm glad to see the POE method converts so well to mathematics.

The feedback I requested from students was a great help. Not only did it let me know what the students were thinking (which was surprisingly different from what I thought they were thinking), but it also let the students know I considered myself and them as a team, working to better *my* teaching and improve *their learning*. I requested feedback once in the middle of the placement and again at the end. The students were not only impressed to be asked for their opinions, but also amazed to see modifications actually *made* from their suggestions (feelings of empowerment). They were also pleased that their opinions were *respected* (plus it gave my classroom management a major edge — student responsibility — especially in the general level class who seem to feel, and in fact often *are*, discounted by the staff — Ouch!!).

The binder dividers were a big help. The mass of paper I was deluged with needed some form of organization and, without the dividers, I don't think I would have known where to start. The only problem I had was that my lesson reviews and journal entries often merged and I wasn't sure which section to include them in. Generally speaking, I felt well prepared for my placement by this course, even though I have difficulty pinpointing exactly *what* it is we've been doing. Interesting irony, there don't you think?

* * * * *

Relationships Are at the Forefront of Learning

I must write things down more — lesson plans and the like. These last three weeks were awesome. One word to describe them would be 'Wow!' I think that I really got to experience what it is like to be a 'teacher' person, to experience the highs and lows, the times with lots of energy, times when you are dragging, the times when things are 'clicking' and those when things are totally haywire. It reaffirmed my belief that relationships are at the forefront of any learning. Your respect and special connections to the students are essential before any learning can take place. I could see very clearly that the students were unique in the way they learned, as they should be, as each of them has come through a different journey and is ultimately a product of parents, friends, teachers, siblings and society. Trying to find a balance to cater to all these different young people made things interesting and exciting every day. Some of their insights into a simple problem or a complicated one were 180 degrees from my own, which was great. They must have taught me a greater bundle about my teaching than I realized before. I think I further found the ability to 'read' people, though I have a way to go. It is an essential part of establishing a comfortable forum where communication can take place. It did take me a while to get 'warmed up,' since it has been a while since the last teaching round. My associate and other teachers also gave me much information on the 'life' of a teacher person.

* * * * *

Reflecting and Writing Showed Me My Strengths and Weaknesses

From the six weeks here [in classes], I got a lot of great ideas and met colleagues whom I could contact in case of need. From the practicum I learned how to put all of these ideas, and my previous experiences, into practice in the classroom. The only way for me to learn my strengths and my weaknesses is to reflect on my teaching, and this is what I did in my placement. I found my associate's comments useful, but my students' comments were often more practical and comforting in a way. They know I'm still learning, so most of them were great about letting me know what would help them learn better.

Getting up in front of the classroom this time seemed to be very different from my previous teaching rounds. I was anxious to get up and teach, rather than continuing to observe my associate. I wanted to see what *I* could do! One factor which was very helpful was that I taught two Grade 11 chemistry classes as well as two Grade 10 science classes (plus an enriched Grade 11 chemistry class from hell!). This meant that I was teaching every lesson twice. I almost always found that my second lesson went better, as I learned where the trouble spots were and how to anticipate any questions that might come up. I also found that my second lesson always took longer, because I was explaining things more fully.

One major factor I noticed was that I was able to relax much more by the last week. I was much more confident with what I was doing and how my students learned best. Both my associates and my students noticed and commented on this. That's all I can think of right now. I'm all written out. It was really good (for me) to be writing journals and comments every day and I'm to the point now where I don't want to do any more! Time to relax!

* * * * *

Observation and Personal Experience Go Hand in Hand

The past three weeks have been filled with experiential learning. For me there were two main parts to my learning.

1 Learning from observation. I learned a lot by observing my associate and other teachers in the department. I was lucky to have the opportunity to be with three different teachers, plus sitting in with two others. I was able to compare and contrast their different teaching styles and the way in which the students responded to the different teaching techniques. Lots of great ideas to try out in step 2.
2 Learning from my own teaching. It is very different to get up in front of a class and teach a lesson from sitting in on a class. Organization: very important to tell kids all housekeeping information at beginning of class plus the plan for the day or week so they know what is coming and what to expect.

Variety keeps a lesson from being boring, especially for a 75-minute class. Checking up on students individually helps to make sure they are on track before formal evaluation.

* * * * *

Meaningful Learning May Require Some Risks

Confidence, Enthusiasm, Rapport, Respect, Relaxed: these are all words to describe my teaching style. They were also key ingredients to success during my round of teaching. Although at times my 'style' got me into hot water, I am excited that I have developed and will continue to develop a distinct style which creates a very positive and sometimes open and unstructured learning atmosphere. I realize from some student reflection (as well as from personal reflection) that modifications could be made to improve on classroom management. However, by taking some risks and sacrificing a little discipline within a sometimes circus-like classroom, a great deal of very meaningful learning went on — and that really excited me. I saw my students taking risks and learning concepts in different ways than they were used to. I really think that in my three weeks I got many — not all — of my students to THINK; that, perhaps, was my biggest accomplishment. My biggest challenge was catering to *all* student needs and abilities — a very tough assignment.

* * * * *

Nothing Could Prepare Me for the Stress of Teaching

Wow! What an intense three weeks! I found the last three weeks very rewarding yet very tiring. My associate teacher was amazing. Our teaching styles were very similar and I couldn't have asked for a better learning environment. Teacher's college did not prepare me for the stress that I would face in those three weeks. I guess you don't really realize how busy you are going to be until you do it.

I did try to do reflections on my teaching each day — something Tom has been pushing — and I could see the growth in my comments over the three weeks. It was fun to read them after the practicum ended — problems I was writing about that seemed so large at the time faded right away. I realized that mistakes were easily fixed.

I feel that we can do a lot of talking here at Queen's but where I really do my true learning is in the classroom. However, these three weeks should help bring up some interesting discussions in our classes as this experience is fresh in our minds. I am looking forward to this time.

* * * * *

Teaching Restored My Faith in Teaching

I have a lot to say about many things today. First, my perception has totally changed. My first two teaching placements [in the concurrent program] didn't really have any significant impact on me, but for some reason — maybe because things seem more real now — this one did. I feel that my thinking about teaching has changed completely. Our classes make a lot more sense now, and I have a million questions.

One thing that really surprised me was how negative some people have been when talking about their practicums, particularly in my computer class. There were only three of us who really loved our experiences. Is this normal? In third year everyone seemed so much more positive. How can we keep our morale up? On another point,

I notice that a lot of people taught in inner-city schools. Most people found it really difficult. I don't have the first clue how I would go about teaching there. What if I get a job in one of them?

I went into the practicum not looking forward to it, and really scared, but this three weeks restored my faith in teaching. My associate teacher was so pumped, so inspired. He made me remember all the reasons I wanted to get into teaching. I had a great experience and am kind of sad it's over. I picked up a lot of things — mostly from making mistakes. I learned what I need to include in my lesson plans. I learned the impact of where I'm standing — lots of classroom management. Techniques/rapport things. I learned just how long 75 minutes can be. You really need to break up the class.

I picked up and also made up many new ideas for how to teach science. I learned a lot from my associate — both in his attitude and in how he taught. It made more sense for me to observe how he taught *after* I'd started teaching than before. Why do we do *all* of our observation at the beginning of our placements? Overall it was great, and I feel a lot better about becoming a teacher.

* * * * *

Teaching Has to Be Organic

My boardwork improved. I realized that my boardwork had to present the material in a way that the students could later learn from, instead of showing my unorganized problem-solving method (where you use any available board space). I guess that is the difference between teaching and working in a Help Centre, solving problems.

The school really impaired the students' ability to learn by messing up their schedules on a weekly basis. I didn't have a single week of normally scheduled days to teach. There was always an event, an assembly, a day off, or a fire drill to give the students shortened periods. There were also many announcements made constantly throughout the day, interrupting the classes.

My associate teacher was funny and easy-going and very helpful. He made lots of jokes in class and believed that any class without some humour was a wasted hour. Regarding the curriculum and the attempt to follow it, he said that 'teaching has to be organic.' It can change from day to day, and your lessons must be as flexible.

* * * * *

Learning to Teach Happens in *the Classroom*

This certainly confirmed the rumours I've heard that most of the learn-ing we do as teachers is *in* the classroom! Many things learned, many frustrations, many nights with too little sleep due to what seemed like massive amounts of preparation. My associate handed the reins over to me from the beginning. As a result of my doing everything myself from scratch, I feel that I learned a lot more about the ups and downs of 'real-life' teaching than I might have otherwise.

However, I paid for it in terms of time to myself, which I had to completely sacrifice in order to attain the level of preparation that I felt the students (and I?) deserved. I have to learn to say 'Enough is enough' with respect to preparation, and allow myself to maintain a life outside of school, and get a decent night's sleep.

Here are the things that helped most from my education classes:

- Doing demos and presentations in front of our class.
- Talking with those who already have some teaching ex-perience about 'do's and don'ts' and lessons they've learned thus far.
- Reading the comments by the pilot project teachers about their experiences [starting to teach on the first day of school].
- Reflecting on the demonstrations we did — what went well and what could be improved upon.

* * * * *

The Learning Is in *the School Experiences*

I definitely feel that the last three weeks were invaluable in terms of the stuff that I learned. For starters, prior to the practicum I was con-vinced that what I really wanted was to teach science, and that teach-ing math was going to be something that I didn't have an intense desire to do. I got into the math classroom three weeks ago and I *loved* it. Now I think that I would be equally happy as a math teacher!! I taught Grade 9 math, Grade 10 math and OAC finite and found that it was a great experience to have a wide variety of ages and ability levels within my classes. It showed how you have to modify your classes and the way that you teach all the time. As a teacher, you probably need to be one of the most flexible people in the world.

In one of my math classes I was able to incorporate POE. I had never really thought of this as something you could do with a math class, but one day there I was doing it and I was really pleased with how well it worked. Using POE in the Grade 9 classroom was different than using it here because at first the students were reluctant to make suggestions, but then once they realized that I wasn't going to say that any ideas were wrong, everyone wanted to give a suggestion, even the weaker kids who rarely spoke up in class. We did it a few times in the same class and with each successive attempt it was more successful. What I had the students do was use a circular-shaped geoboard to establish the different angles and relationships within the circle. Each time we guessed what the relationships could possibly be and put them all up on the board. I was showing them the angles that they should be measuring on a clear geoboard which was on an overhead projector. Then they would have to build the kinds of angles we were investigating, measure them and establish which relationships were correct. The kids seemed to enjoy this and I would definitely use this strategy again!

I learned a lot from my associate's comments, the students' comments and from trying things that I never thought I would try (i.e., POE, using computer programs, etc.). I also learned from the professional development day conference that I had the chance to attend. All of the teachers who presented were very dynamic and organized interactive workshops that we could participate in and learn from. One of my workshops was on a computer program called 'Authority' and the other was on math waves and graphing calculators. Neat stuff!!

Only by being in the school, I discovered, can you learn how many different types of students there really are and how much the situation at home affects the student's ability to learn. One student in particular is repeating Grade 9 this year and is experiencing major difficulties. When my associate contacted the student's mother to arrange a meeting where they could evaluate her son's needs and develop a plan for success, she carried on extensively about how her son doesn't want to learn and the teachers should not continue to waste their time on him. She even went so far as to say that the taxpayers and government were wasting their money on her son's education. The strange thing is that this particular student *does* try and seems to want to learn. He comes in almost every day for help but has minimal ability. I couldn't believe the kinds of things the mother was saying and probably wouldn't have believed it if I hadn't heard about it first hand. What can you do for this kind of student who so obviously has no support from the home. Understanding the varying degrees of support students get from the home and how it affects their learning is something that we can only learn from experience.

Some of the things that we discussed in our curriculum courses at Queen's were incorporated into my classes while out in my practicum. I think, however, that having the specific context of the classroom made it just happen naturally. For instance, the day that I did POE I had not set out with this in mind, but it just came to me. On the whole, I would say that some of the things I learned at Queen's were useful and remained in the back of my mind, but the real learning came from the classroom experience of the last three weeks.

* * * * *

Practice Helps, Yet Reality Can Be So Different

I think that, no matter how you approach it, real learning about teaching does not occur until you are out there with thirty or so students in front of you. For example, it is one thing to be psychologically prepared to be in front of people but quite another thing to actually be there at the centre of the stage. We may talk about situations that may occur in the classroom and how to deal with them, but in real life things may be very different. I think that the one-year education program for the consecutive students could be better if the teaching rounds were longer, and if one were to assume a gradually more responsible role instead of being responsible for everything right from the very beginning. Practicing lesson planning and seeing actual models of it may be a great help for me. Also, ways to cope with all kinds of students (bright and dull) and have them busy and challenged at all times could be reviewed at Queen's. For example, what should you do if you assign seat work and the bright students are done in 10 minutes, whereas most of the class need 20 minutes, or if you give them a test and 20 per cent of the students are done in half the time, what would you do with them? How do you keep on top of your lesson if the 'bright' student is constantly asking you for clarification? You seem to be running the class just for the bright. How to motivate students could be one thing we review at the faculty.

* * * * *

Sharing Our Experiences Is Very Worthwhile

Unfortunately, I didn't get to practice teach the past three weeks. Thus I wasn't able to determine whether or not the handouts you've given out are useful or not. However, there are certain things that I'd like to comment on.

First, for me at least, the most worthwhile experience of all at Queen's is being in an environment with other prospective teachers. It's comforting and educational. For instance, today just listening to others talk about their teaching round illustrates once again the variety of *different* teachers, students and schools that are out there. At the same time there is an artificiality to Queen's — it's not so much this course, but having all kinds of assignments that have to be done in the next four weeks seems ridiculous. I'm not sure how those assignments are going to help me in the following four months [when I will be teaching]. I would much rather discuss, discuss again, research what I'd like, and go and see the professor as I need to. Anyway, enough venting.

I'm convinced (from previous experience) that my actual learning is going to take place in the classroom. Frankly, I'm frightened that I may be responsible for teaching classes pretty much from the beginning of the second semester, and some of the students need their marks for university admissions. But I'll have to deal with whatever comes at that time.

The Voice of a Poet Learning to Teach, 2

Tanya Marwitz

Ballet Dancer

she takes her place and is ready to begin
the ring of the bells signal her start
graceful and confident, she floats around the room
reciting the words of a well-known part

each angel she passes is blessed with her smile
her footsteps unheard as she leaps and turns
years of choreography lie in every step
but, always, she finds something new to learn

after years of practice, she may still drop her wand
and, at times, she is seen bumping into a prop
but the angels are patient with knowing smiles
they sense her humanity and never ask her to stop

the dance is a ritual, but never the same
each day brings new movements to a well-known routine
her body and mind are united in purpose
but the struggles she's suffered go often unseen

her world is bears and rainbows and pumpkins
Santas and stars and snakes galore
but always the angels her reason for dancing
despite disapproval from the ogres next door

(September 1996 — inspired by my associate teacher,
whose grace in this profession has been apparent
from the start)

Chapter 5

Voices from Eight Weeks of Teaching

Overview

The voices in this chapter are drawn from the group of sixty-two
teacher candidates in a 'pilot project' testing a new teacher education
program structure at Queen's University. These individuals volunteered
for early extended teaching experience. They also volunteered to prepare these accounts of what it is like to learn from extended experience.

Some have been enrolled in education courses since beginning
their undergraduate studies, at Queen's University or at Trent University,
and they have had several brief teaching opportunities in earlier years.
Others volunteered for early teaching even though they had not previously experienced any formal introduction to teaching. All attended
a week-long orientation period prior to being in their assigned schools
on the opening day of the school year. After eight weeks of teaching,
they returned to the university for two weeks of classes and discussions,
and at that time they were invited to prepare contributions to this
collection of new teachers' voices. These accounts are from both
elementary and secondary teachers, and they cover the full range of
familiar topics related to teaching and learning to teach.

A World of Possibilities
Tanya Marwitz

It's Hallowe'en. For children in primary grades, this is the day they've
been working towards since the last mouthful of cranberries and turkey
was swallowed on October 14th. For me, a member of Queen's Pilot
Program, it was a day that had lost a little of its shine from being away
from the classroom for the last four school days, while attending the
professional discussions at McArthur Hall. That is, the shine was lost
until this afternoon when I set foot in the school that has been my
second home for the last eight weeks.

Once she got past the yellow, sunflower-looking balloons that
circled my face, one of 'my' Grade 1 students came running down the
hall with arms outstretched, eyes sparkling and a simple cry, 'Miss

Marwitz, you're BACK!!!!' A powerful hug followed and I knew for certain that I had accomplished something wonderful since September 3rd, 1996. The unsolicited whispers of 'I really missed you' as a particular student wrapped his arms around my waist spoke volumes of the impression I had made upon him and his peers as their 'second' teacher.

In this pilot program, one of the fundamental changes is the placement of teacher candidates in their associate schools for an extended experience which commences on the first day of school. We are placed with a *school*, as opposed to a classroom, to our great advantage. The staff and students come to know us as part of their community, a familiar face that is seen on the playgrounds, around the staff room and in the assemblies. When my placement concludes, I will have spent fourteen weeks in three different grade levels, learning all that I am capable of absorbing from a variety of professionals. More importantly, in my opinion, I will also have had the privilege of learning so many lessons from the students themselves.

What strikes me as so fundamentally valuable about this — and all — teaching experience is the potential to see possibilities that were previously unimagined. Students at any age enter the classroom with a single, unspoken expectation: to be guided by a teacher who will make the learning process engaging and relevant enough to encourage life-long learning, both in and out of the classroom. These may sound like large shoes to fill, but any teachers who respect and truly *listen* to their students will find themselves on the path towards that goal.

I spent eight weeks in the company of an outstanding associate whose first words of guidance were extremely empowering: 'We are a *team* in this classroom.' These weeks were equally turbulent and inspiring as we juggled the dual challenges of meeting individual *and* collective needs and interests in our classroom. We struggled together against bureaucratic challenges over integration and we triumphed alongside every child who discovered the thrill of being able to read and print for the first time. From the very first day, these children embraced me as a teacher in the room to whom they could come with questions *and* answers. This is where the notion of possibility and the freedom it brings were brought to my attention.

The details of each 'lesson plan' were never formulated more than one or two days in advance. The questions that were interspersed with my story-reading were never written on paper beforehand. The art 'lessons' rarely had my product as a model. To some, this may sound like a classroom of chaos and disorganization. I would argue that this classroom was built upon an ever-changing structure of possibilities. With questions like 'What *could* this be?', not 'What *is* this?', I was able to be an audience to nineteen voices of expertise and reasoning, each with a unique perspective and a surprising tone of logic at the age of 6 that made all answers possible and each child valued. Granted, there were occasions when only one answer to 'two plus two' was supported, but the majority of answers to any question I posed came from the students' diverse perspectives, not mine.

Their voices gave dimension to story book illustrations and their eyes saw details and inconsistencies that a teacher rushing through pre-formatted lessons would often miss. They were forthcoming with their answers, knowing that I would listen and appreciate them. Their ultra-sensitive 'radar' for truth and justice could spot insincerity a mile away, so I was adamant about being honest through every moment we were together.

I didn't know if blue whales were actually blue. I didn't always remember where I'd left the masking tape. I wasn't always sure what equipment I would have ready for physical education until we got to the gym. I didn't have to know. My students were always watching and it actually made my job so much *easier* and much more valuable for the students. Trusting *them* with many aspects of classroom life gave them confidence. Encouraging my students to choose activities and to select songs and games that *they* enjoyed made them willing participants in each day's schedule.

I much prefer being a fallible human being than a seemingly all-knowing sage who is always scrambling to be ahead of my students. A lot of what my colleagues seem to be stressed about would easily dissolve if they weren't so consumed with being 'in control' every minute of the school day. At 6 years old, my students didn't need two adults constantly circling the room during activities. One of us was present at all times if they were in need of direction, but their ability to self-direct and to gain whatever each of them needed from the activities increased daily. I encouraged their independence in thought and action and they returned ten-fold with respect for their classroom community to which each of us, student and teacher alike, was accountable.

I can say, with some confidence and a glance at my tracking sheets, that these Grade 1 students learned a great deal during the eight weeks that I shared their classroom. However, it gives me greater pride to say that I learned so much more from *them* while I was there. They proved to me that possibilities become endless when voices are encouraged rather than stifled. And, today, they showed me a new mathematical equation: one hug from a grateful child is greater than any frustration encountered in one's classroom.

Room to Grow
Andrew Cotton

As I peered at the playing children through the window of room 4, I became conscious immediately of how the window symbolized the uniqueness of my position as a teacher candidate. Although a window separates people, it does not close us off from one another, but rather invites us to share and witness diverse experiences. Standing on the other side of the classroom window, I am separate from the students yet the clear panes allow me to identify with them. As teacher candidate, I too am a student — a student of teaching. Yet here, on the first day, by all external appearances I will be introduced and perceived as a fellow teacher by both students and staff. As the clock ticked closer and closer to 9 o'clock, questions that had always been with me now seemed louder, more colourful, more urgent. *Will I be able to teach these children?* Have my own life lessons been of enough value to aid these young people? Are my strengths great enough to overshadow my weaknesses and insecurities? Most importantly, *can I transform these personal strengths into tools for great teaching?*

As twenty-one little bodies marched past me into the room, I am sure my expression mirrored theirs — wide-eyed, hesitant, and nervous. Once again, my commonalities with the students outweighed the differences. I was introduced by my associate teacher in the most generous manner possible. She said: 'There are two teachers in this class: Mrs W___ and Mr Cotton.' What music to my ears! After years of feeling like a guest in another's classroom, here in room 4 the expectation had already been established that I was to be treated with the same respect as a full teacher, and that I too had to fulfill these responsibilities. This first day I watched as Mrs W___ introduced routines, procedures and expectations within the classroom. In so doing, I was better able to address my concerns about starting my own classroom on the first day of school. For the first two days, I was a silent observer in the classroom. I studied the students and their interactions with each other and the teacher. What did they respond to? As I eavesdropped on their conversations, I made note of subjects that were of interest to them. Similarly, I stalked my associate, quietly writing down her tactics for classroom management that have withstood years of teaching. *Would these methods work for me?*

The question that popped into my head on the first day was double-edged. As a student of teaching, I believe many of us must overcome fears of losing control in the classroom, and as we struggle to contain this fear, we readily embrace techniques modeled before us, grabbing at them as we would a life preserver in a raging sea. Yet, as I ponder this question, 'Would her methods work for me?', I cannot help but wonder if I would drown anyway, silencing my own voice within the classroom. Like a sponge, I want to savour my associate's years of experience and avoid costly mistakes that could impede a child's learning, but how do I reconcile this with my place in the classroom? How do I avoid being co-opted into the existing educational system? Without formal teacher training preceding this practicum, would the absence of theory be an invitation to adopt poor teaching habits? Although we were provided with introductory sessions that acquainted us with curriculum documents and introduced us to our field-based courses on inclusion, equity and legal issues, as well as professional theory and practice, many still wondered if we would become effective educators without professional instruction.

Room to grow. Although it sounds like the title of a magazine's decorating section about kids' bedrooms, it means much more to me. After years of guiding and educating pre-service teachers, my associate believes that the best teacher preparation is *practice, practice, practice.* On the third day I was no longer silent; I read stories to the class. On the fourth day I was introducing a spelling lesson. Like a baby's first steps learning to walk, my first teaching steps were incremental. To paraphrase my associate's words, you can observe a teacher as long as you want, but until you are in front of that classroom, you won't be prepared for teaching. As I quickly learned, students will take a lesson in a direction you had not planned. I learned how to read the class, becoming increasingly aware that a class has its own rhythms, that each individual child contributes a special dynamic to the class and that each child's presence or absence influences the tone of that school day. Most importantly, I am continuing to learn how to adapt my lessons to the chameleon-like quality of the classroom. Each day this entity of energy, laughter and tantrums presents a different face to me and as my baby steps become bigger and more stable, I nevertheless have moments when I fall. And falling down is OK. In falling down, I learn more about myself than I ever could in a classroom at the Faculty of Education. *It all comes back to my associate giving me room to grow.* She is a willing counsel and ready advisor on all my lessons, my thoughts and my observations, but most significantly, she has given me the freedom to grow and to make my own mistakes.

Such experience has given me confidence. Unlike the teacher candidates who remained at the Faculty of Education during the Fall term, teaching for just three weeks, I have lived, breathed and witnessed issues of inclusion, equity, and legality in schools. I haven't sat down and hypothesized about events in schools. Instead, each day has been a lesson in itself. Children, as we know, are not static but ever-changing beings. Teacher candidates, similarly, are developing professionally with each new classroom scenario; the relationship is symbiotic. As we try to address children's diverse needs, they are addressing our needs for teaching preparation as well. *My voice as a teacher person is becoming more audible.* I have taken the benefit of my associate's years of experience and my short classroom placements in earlier years and combined them with my own philosophy of teaching. I am so far from being where I want to be as an educator, yet I feel I am well on my way. I know that I want to be a facilitator of the learning process, a sleuth in finding a child's interest and then building upon it, making learning pertinent in their lives.

As I look out the window, once again I see myself in harmony with my students. They are growing in every way possible. Physically, I can see a difference in them. While some of them are taller, others are maturing through their willingness to work at their studies. I too have changed. At one time I was worried about how I was going to handle the class, but after eight weeks my needs are no longer the principal concern. Instead, my focus is on *their* learning — what are the best methods to facilitate *their* diverse learning needs? This progression, and I do believe it is a progression, is an unconscious one. Somewhere along the way, I switched from the mentality of teacher-candidate to that of teacher. Only now, as I 'speak' to my computer screen, am I conscious of the changes in my own agenda since September. *I am responsible for the learning of these children.* The children in room 4 have become *our* students, not simply her students. Although there is so much more that I need and want to know about becoming a successful teacher, the last two months have provided the best preparation possible. If 'all the world's a stage,' then within the classroom we are all unscripted actors. I have found there is no single way to become a successful teacher. Instead, we rely on taking cues from our pupils and our peers. This unscripted, unrehearsed performance is the most significant performance of our professional lives.

Starting to Teach: Will I Sink or Swim?
Anna Haras

Many people take lessons to help them learn a new skill; this seems only logical. However, not everyone adopts this safe approach; some people prefer to jump right in. Usually, I would group myself with those who take lessons first, yet this September I found myself in a 'sink-or-swim' situation. Was I becoming a risk-taker? On September 3, 1996, I embarked on an eight-week practicum in which I would take on the role of teacher without any formal training. The first day of school for the students would also be my first day as a teacher. What was I thinking? Although I am not a natural risk-taker, I am a firm believer that you learn best by doing. Thus I had faith that my years as a student would convey some natural ability to 'swim.'

For the first week of school I was assigned by the principal to various classes (Grade 5/6 and Grade 2/3), and I became a keen observer. I saw the various teaching styles of experienced teachers and the different attitudes of students. My observations told me that what was 'real' was very different from what I anticipated it would be. For example, a parent will drop off and pick up a child, and I had interpreted this as a normal event. Then the experienced teachers explained that this is usually done to prevent the non-custody parent from kidnapping the child. Wow! — my naiveté about the various elements of 'swimming' was shattered!

Over the next seven weeks I became part of a Grade 3/4 class (8- and 9-year-olds) of twenty-eight students — six girls and twenty-two boys! My associate teacher's approach was based on success, and she took on the role of coach and cheerleader. I was quickly assigned the task of preparing and teaching lessons in my favourite subjects. My associate felt that if you have a passion for something the students will feel that passion and go on to develop their own appreciation for it as well. Having had many successful experiences in Art and Physical Education, I tend to agree with her theory. It is great to start by teaching what you know and what interests you. My anxiety and nervousness faded quickly, and soon I didn't even notice my associate teacher sitting at the back of the class. All I saw were twenty-eight pairs of twinkling eyes! This was an awesome feeling — a little frightening, yet also challenging — to realize that I was swimming rather than sinking.

Initially, I was careful to make detailed lesson plans that I would be able to follow as I taught. My 'coach' had told me that you always need a game plan, but I soon learned that things are never so simple. Flexibility and being able to think on your feet are 'where it's at' in an integrated elementary classroom. In gym class, what you think takes five minutes takes at least fifteen, and what you think takes fifteen minutes may take only five.

I have also learned that there are no easy formulas when it comes to classroom management techniques and skills. What works once doesn't always work twice. The advice from my associate teacher was, 'Be consistent and firm and the students will come around. You'll eventually find your personal style.' She told me that each year her style changes to fit the pupils in her class. As a teacher candidate I felt fortunate to witness the chaos before routines were established. It is comforting to know that classroom management is one of those things that has no one right answer or method, even though you desperately wish it did. New teachers encounter many classroom management problems that frustrate us, but we learn from these experiences and move on. The waves are just part of the process of improving your swimming.

My Roller-coaster Ride with a Grade 4–5 Class
Christa Armstrong

The first eleven weeks of my teacher education program have been quite an interesting experience! Children have always fascinated me, but I had never had the experience of teaching and learning with a group of thirty individuals before. I was scared, excited and (in hindsight) idealistic. The truth is that I continue to operate with this mixed bag of emotions, but underneath it all I love it! It took involvement with children in numerous contexts before I realized that I actually wanted to teach. It had been my challenge for years to work with 'at-risk' individuals. For one year I had the privilege of working with street children in Ecuador, and for two summers I felt the joy of affiliation with children from Harlem, New York. As a Canadian I was interested in engagement with similar children in my own country. The children in each country I have worked with come from very poor economic backgrounds. My career was beginning to define itself. It seemed a natural progression to advance into the world of teaching. I had no idea when I first began how huge that world actually is.

My first day of teaching finally arrived and I embarked on a completely foreign adventure. There I was in the Grade 4–5 classroom, teaching 9- and 10-year-olds. I was nervous on the inside; I hoped I was calm on the outside. I was very aware of that fact that I get red in the face quite easily. When reading the children a story, I tried as hard as I could to make sure this face of mine was not turning red, and hopefully I succeeded. If any of the children noticed my flushing, they were kind souls not to mention it!

I knew I was in my element when one of the children got into a lot of trouble. The child had displayed considerable aggression, frustration and confusion, and he got himself into a fight. This was a new one for my teacher, because fighting did not generally begin on the first day of the school year. I was completely unsure about how many of the techniques I had learned were feasible in a classroom. As this young boy was actually choking another child, I quickly figured out the first step of ending the confrontation immediately. So many of the actions, concerns, and dilemmas matched my past experiences, yet here I was in a different position. Incidents such as this reminded me of all the things I still have to learn about teaching. There are books to read and procedures to follow. Who was I to step into some of the larger issues developing in the school? Ignorance is not always bliss. The child was soon expelled from the school and sent to a local children's centre that focuses on behaviour management. This was a new solution for me, as the organizations I had worked with outside Canada did not have support schools and the children lacked the option of moving elsewhere.

It took me some time to allow more and more of myself into the classroom. My prior knowledge of children could help me and I needed to listen to my previous experiences. The principles I had developed were limited, but they were all I had. I believe that one must personally finish everything one starts with a child. Do not 'start' things with children, and this means avoiding a threat dance — the aggressive tango that only leads you back and forth until you attempt to follow up a threat. Be honest and open with children. Attempt to employ humour and use the scores of behaviour modification techniques which do not involve yelling. I just do not like to yell, especially when I would rather laugh! Observe and know your children so you can see problems arising and then deal with them on the spot, rather than when the fists come up. Keep them so busy that they simply have no time to fight. On a more dishonest note, make them believe you know everything and have superheroine powers of seeing out of the eyes in the back of your head. When I was a student, I was certainly no angel, but I did respect the teachers who respected me. It remains my contention that respect is not given: respect is something to be earned. Earning the respect of all children I work with is crucial.

The issue of fighting was removed from our class. Naturally, there was the odd 'clash of the titans,' but none so brutal as on the first day. What does it mean to speak of 'inner-city living' and 'low socioeconomic backgrounds'? What do those words mean? Why are so many of the same issues apparent in any country? To be fair to Ecuador, it was the least violent of the three countries I have worked in. The longer I work at a school, the more clearly I can see beneath its fabric. All schools are busy, and no one has the time to tell us what to do, yet it does not take long to see everything that needs to be done. My school has a snack program and a lunch program, with teachers and educational assistants working above and beyond the call of duty.

Our school has high needs in both academic and social terms. One child arrives late to school nearly every day, and I happened to overhear her mother say to her one day, 'I'm going to kick your ass!' How I wish that all my students received a kiss or a hug rather than a threat at the start of the day. When I asked another student why she had been absent, she told me that her mother will not let her go to school when her mother is ill. I was not sure I had heard the child correctly. (Sometimes I seem to need people to explain things to me as though I'm a 5-year-old.) Speaking slowly and in smaller words, her claim remained the same. What do I do or say in such a case? A school colleague suggested a simple call home, noting that the child's absence was the best place to start. The call could indicate to all concerned that the absence of the child had been noticed and considered important.

I was shocked to discover that one of the children in the Grade 5 is reading at a Grade 1 level. How could this happen? It seemed outrageous. This boy was gracious enough to allow me to work with him, and our first week together enabled us to get to know each other, figure out what we wanted to accomplish, and determine if there were any reading difficulties that could be tracked. We both agreed that learning to read would be great. It was difficult to judge his actual reading ability because of his complete lack of confidence. From the books I took in, he always chose one with the fewest and smallest words. He would scrutinize each book, but not for the interesting pictures or the great plot. Reading more about different learning styles gave me some strategies and approaches to developing language skills. The more I got to know him, the more I realized how much he could help both of us by going to bed before 1 o'clock in the morning! We tried several strategies. Many days he was not in the mood to work but he began to understand that our time together was not going to be wasted on my chasing him to work. At one point I was quite surprised when we renegotiated our weekly schedule. I wanted to know if he would prefer to work three days a week as opposed to five, and he made it clear that our schedule should remain at five days a week. There was a period when I wondered if our work was going anywhere. I was so excited when he started to show progress! My enthusiasm hit a brick wall when he was tested and the 'expert' declared that he would probably never read beyond the Grade 3 level. I prefer to believe that he might have done poorly that day because of his self-consciousness. Perhaps some great television program the night before kept him up very late. Perhaps I am naive to doubt all testing. At this stage in the game, idealism can actually work as a great source of energy and motivation. I worry now that his progress may be lost as I move into another classroom to continue my teaching.

The classroom is completely action-packed — an exciting and exhausting place to be. At times I still marvel that I am actually allowed to be responsible for thirty children. Upon reflection I do not know what I am doing all day, but it seems to be working. There are some subjects that I love teaching and others for which I need to go to the library and use other people's great ideas. I was astonished to learn how many different ways a person could actually teach spelling, and it became painfully apparent to me that I could use a complete course just on blackboard skills. I loved the children in my first class, but saying that does not mean they were angels. On the contrary, they took me on a daily roller-coaster ride. At times they took us to the top of the ride, high in the clouds, yet on other days we went speeding down with no end in sight. They are an intense, high energy group of individuals, and it was a joy to work with them.

Teaching to Learn, Learning to Teach
Jennifer Crits

Teaching is really a learning process and, as I have just discovered, the best way to learn how to teach is by doing it. It may seem difficult to imagine that a Bachelor of Education intern could be sent off on a four-month mission to teach school with relatively no previous experience or training, yet my pilot-project colleagues and I did it and learned that it works!

After one week of intense studies at Queen's, we headed out to face the first day of school. Were we nervous? Yes. Scared? Definitely. But that first day of school became the foundation for the 'wall of authority and confidence' that we, as developing professionals, had set out to build. It was on the first day of the school year that all the students met both their new teachers — the associate teacher and the intern (me!). Instead of having only one teacher, the children have two. They did not see my associate teacher as the one in charge; we were both seen as equal figures of authority. In this way I began to gain confidence in managing the classroom, in teaching, and in fulfilling the role of a teacher.

As the weeks of the practicum continued, my confidence level increased as my teaching experiences broadened. My classroom activity increased steadily as I took on the responsibility of helping to ensure the success — socially, academically and emotionally — of each child in the class. My authority was being established by my active presence in the classroom, in the school, in the lunchroom and at extracurricular events. I attempted to model the behaviour and the appearance of a professional, and through these the students respected me as a source of authority.

After five weeks, I left my Grade 1/2 class and went to teach in a self-contained 'adjustment' classroom for children aged 9 to 11. At first I wondered what I had to offer the students in this regimented and highly structured classroom. I felt awkward and useless until I taught — with fear and trembling — my first French lesson. It was a total success, and I realized I did have something unique to offer these exceptional children. Taught in a manner suited to their needs and interests, they responded positively and my sense of confidence increased. I went home saying over and over, 'They learned! I succeeded!' The five members of the class began to trust me. I believed in them and they, in turn, believed in me.

This gave me the confidence to press on, even though there were days when lessons flopped and the boys became frustrated and angry. I often spent time reflecting back on the lesson. What could I have done differently so that the learning would have been more effective? Reflection allowed me to see things from different perspectives and to get helpful opinions from other professionals. I began to see what a valuable tool reflection could be in my process of learning how to become a better teacher. All these experiences, some positive and some negative, have been stepping stones in my journey of professional development, each step serving to increase my confidence and ease at managing a classroom and feeling more secure in my role as a teacher. These four months have clearly been a successful learning experience in my professional life.

In Search of the Golden Answer
C. Katy Bittenbinder

It sounds corny, but I'll admit it! Occasionally, I find myself day-dreaming about teaching an unprecedented 'great lesson.' In my little fantasy world, my lessons are profound and articulate, and all the students are enthralled with the knowledge that I am bestowing upon them. My day-dream is probably tightly linked to the fact that I set my goal years ago to become a teacher. I am captivated by the challenge of teaching kids. I embrace the opportunity to know them and to learn from and with them. Unfortunately, my perfect little day-dream fell from its height during my eight-week teaching assignment.

My first few days in school were fun. It was the beginning of the school year, when everyone is caught up in a whirlwind of potential for what the year ahead may bring. The students were interested in me, my role in their class, what sports I played in high school, how old I am, if I knew their older brother now in his first year at Queen's, why would I ever *want* to be a teacher, if I was sexually active, if I'd buy them beer? You name it, they asked it — quite literally! I observed (and was questioned non-stop) for the first few days. I sat up at the front of the class and, like a model student, I took precise notes on how my associate teacher established the 'ground rules.' It was easy. It was too easy.

On the day when I finally got up and spoke, my voice simply refused to work for me. What I said came out in a muddled mush. My visions of being the great, articulate and profound teacher fell into a pile of self-consciousness and uncertainty about what I was saying. I did the worst things possible. I asked them, 'Would you like to do this activity?' and quite naturally I heard from those who did not. During my lectures, I asked them, 'Are you with me?', and looked around the class to discover blank stares and looks of severe boredom. My most hellish realization came as I was teaching a lesson on writing essays and I realized that I was bored by my own teaching! Ouch! Learning to teach became difficult and overwhelming. How could I teach when the students would rather be any place else than in my class? I'd always thought that somehow they would just want to be there. All the pre-paration I had done had not prepared me for this. There was just too much to think about — what to say, how to say it clearly and precisely, what to move to next, when to move on, how to ask the right ques-tions, how to handle the 'behaviour problems,' how to entertain the students, how to motivate them, how to actually have fun myself when I had to think about all these other things.

Just before the beginning of the school year, in one of my 'orien-tation' classes at the Faculty of Education, we developed a list of char-acteristics that define a teacher. One person suggested that a teacher is a 'gardener.' At the time, I loved this metaphor, which seemed both accurate and poetic. Now, beyond the fact that both occupations are very messy, I no longer see the similarities. We are not cultivating young minds, we are boring them. We are trying to 'keep them on track.' We are just trying to survive. We are not gardeners, we are fire jugglers, trying to smile and entertain while terrified to death that we'll catch the stick with the lit end. Juggling takes a lot of practice. Every minute of teaching I have to account for about 100 different things — the students who missed the last class, the constant interruptions, the mood of the student, individual learning needs, individual emotional needs, actually teaching them something, remembering what I am teaching, getting everything covered that they need, thinking about what I'm going to do or say next, and trying my hardest not to bore them. Ahhhh!

When there are so many things to do or think about, some aspects just have to suffer. I decided to start working on how not to bore my students. So I tried to spice up my lesson, presenting it to them as though it was the greatest idea anyone ever had. I imagined that if they weren't bored, there wouldn't be any 'discipline problems.' But in order for things to work and to keep everyone engaged, I still had to keep control. (There are a few kids, I have learned, whom I have to keep one eye on at all times.) With all of my energy invested in the presentation, and with my eyes crossed to cover all the bases, I find that my patience is low for dealing with their reactions to my ideas (whether they are enthusiastic about them or not). Every once in a while, as I am desperately trying to manage their energy, I notice a twinge of 'that tone' in my voice. I am horrified every time I hear that 'You won't know what to do unless you all listen' teacher tone of voice. The scariest thing of all about 'that tone' is that *it works*! It may work, but I don't want to use it. I know that I must find an alternative. I hate myself for using it and I hate that tone every time I hear it.

I still have not found the golden answer. More importantly, I've realized that there probably isn't one. What has worked for me is forgetting myself and having fun. Then I realize that the odd, small interruption isn't really that big a deal. Amazingly enough, when I genuinely have fun, so do my students. My best days are those when I laugh sincerely, tell stories about myself, and worry less. On one particular day, in one of these particular moods, I noticed a student yawn. She quickly and politely tried to hide the fact that she was yawning. I told the class the story about a professor I had in university who felt that our society is too preoccupied with yawning, which is simply a basic human response to needing more oxygen in our lungs. If anyone yawned in her class, she would respond with a cheerful, 'Good for you!' I told this story, and the class continued. A few weeks later, when I was feeling particularly tired, I yawned on the sly. A boy in the class promptly bellowed out, 'Good for you!', and I was shocked! I laughed, but most of all I was extremely impressed. He had listened! I had told him something that he remembered! I basked in my moment of revelation that I had actually taught this boy something. This made me realize that I shouldn't worry so much that they are not 'getting it.' If I relax and be the teacher that I've always day-dreamed I could be, they will *actually* learn something. If they yawn, they could be bored, but more likely they just need more oxygen in their lungs. I continue to be enchanted by the challenge.

Experience First!
Lisa Borovskis

If you expect to be a good teacher, the ability to teach is a skill you should possess even before you are ever told how to teach. Teaching is about who you are, what things are important to you, and how you feel about other people and society. If you have completed an undergraduate degree, you should have the academic knowledge to educate other people. The problem with teaching is not, 'What am I teaching?', but rather, 'How do I successfully teach?' In a formal training session, a new teacher may be told about certain methods or ideas to aid in the teaching process but a pre-service teacher can only really learn from a classroom setting with authentic students. This is why an introductory teaching placement enables teaching candidates to begin their true learning processes right from the first day.

On the first day that I was actually teaching my class, things did not go as well as I had planned. I am only a few years older than the students I was teaching, and I did not feel like a respected authority figure. I was so focused on knowing the material and being ready to handle students' questions that I wasn't properly attending to the students' behaviours. With my mind fixed firmly on the material, I didn't notice who was listening, who was falling behind, and who needed extra stimulation. After my first attempt as a teacher, I was very critical of myself and I wanted to try again right away, making improvements to my lessons. Every lesson and every class that a teacher experiences with students is a learning event that produces ideas for improvement and for reassurance about successful methods.

I always thought that knowing as much as possible about my teaching subject was the key to my future success as a teacher. In front of my class I quickly learned that, while a thorough knowledge of a topic is important, it is also the easiest part of a teacher's job. A teacher must be able to see each student as an individual having a complex life consisting of stresses, problems, relationships and the many concerns any of us has. Dealing with an enraged student or a socially introverted student may be part of a typical day in a teacher's life. Some students bring heavy issues and burdens with them to school every day, and a teacher must be able to attend to a student's individual needs.

Every day that I have spent as a teacher has made me a better person, more confident that I am in the correct profession. Teachers face enormous challenges day after day, and they must be continuous learners themselves. Teachers are rewarded not by money or recognition but rather by knowing that they have helped their students become better individuals.

Teaching without Formal Training: I Love It!
LizAnn Kliewer

My first day as a 'real' teacher was the first day of the school year. After one week of orientation classes on curriculum, critical issues and professionalism, I was sent out to teach for eight weeks. Images of 'entering into combat without basic weapons training' flashed through my mind. I envisioned hordes of children laughing at me as they realized this student teacher had no clue what she was talking about. Pandemonium would ensue. The faculty would find a clerical error with my acceptance and I would be sent packing before the first recess bell could ring. I had been a tutor, a coach, an ESL instructor, a guide . . . but no one had ever taught me to be a teacher. Who came up with this scheme? Why was I paying tuition to take part in something I would stumble through?

Without many theories to draw upon, I found myself racking the depths of my mind to think of ways to get my students involved and interested in their learning. Since I did not know the theory of what to expect, I looked to them to show me. For the first few days in my class, I was completely caught up in observing the students — their interactions with each other and the teacher, their reactions to instructions and activities, their moods and their needs. At times, I would ask my associate teacher's interpretation of an activity or of a student's work. Open and articulate, she would give me her views and ask about my own. My views were not restricted by things I had read about children in Grade 3 or by a professor's vision of 8-year-olds and how they should be taught. The more time I spent in the class, the stronger my own educational vision became.

Reality struck early. Not having classes on teaching exceptional children did not stop me from developing lessons to include them. The challenges I faced were real and immediate. Students are not 'What ifs?' Much teaching comes from knowing how to 'teach on your feet' — being able to adapt plans at a moment's notice when the class is curious to explore a different avenue, when resources suddenly become unavailable, or when the fire alarm rings. I viewed my placement as a chance to see what the system could offer me that worked and what I wanted to change.

While I have been told that academics in education often worry that new teachers will be 'co-opted' by existing school practices, I find myself very attentive to what might be changed in schools. Why didn't I feel pulled into the system when I had little academic training to support my personal views? Why did my initial sense of nervousness not translate into a desire to fit in and conform? Beginning teachers have a unique perspective on the profession that they are just starting to find their place in. To reach this point in my life, I had already been a part of the system for years. Now I was taking on a new role in a very familiar system. My own experiences as a student were only part of my decision to become a teacher. Before I re-entered the school system as a beginning teacher, I had worked in other fields and experienced life outside the school. Entering the classroom, I brought more than just a desire to become a teacher. I brought a willingness to learn, to make mistakes and to strive for excellence.

During those first few weeks as a fledgling professional, I began to learn theories, concepts and strategies. I also learned about circumstances, personalities and dynamics. The latter forced me to confront my ideals about classes, schools and teachers. These are issues that have pushed me to question my vision of education, and also to question the status quo in schools. Theories and policies do not always translate well into reality. When someone asks me now how I feel about inclusive practices for children with special needs, I do not answer in 'What ifs?,' I answer with reality. Being in a class, observing students and teaching them without the baggage of 'shoulds' and 'musts' is a remarkable experience. It has opened me up to risking myself, my ideas, my vision. I can't wait to return to 'my' school for another six weeks with a brand-new group of children.

The Challenge of Learning to Teach
Nancy J. Berndt

During my Orientation Week at the university, we were told to 'expect the unexpected.' Little did I know that we should expect *only* the unexpected! I was both excited and nervous to be starting my four-month teaching internship. My other educational placements had been confined to only two weeks each. To be facing four months at only one school seemed a daunting task. I knew that in the long run this would be a great experience, since it would prepare me for my own classroom and enable me to follow secondary school students through almost a complete semester.

This first week was a chance for me to get to know my associate teachers, students and school, as well as an opportunity to choose the classes in which I would spend the majority of my time. I ended up choosing a Grade 10 art class, a Grade 9 social science class, and a Grade 11 ancient civilizations class. It took me until part of the way through the second week of school to finally learn all the students' names and, of course, the easiest names to learn were those of the students who misbehaved!

During the first few weeks I found it fascinating to watch my social science associate gain control over the Grade 9 class. On the very first day of school I was in the classroom and my associate left the room just for an instant. Before I knew it, one student was chasing another out the door of the classroom. Without thinking, my old lifeguard instincts kicked in and I was able to stop the second student from running after the first and then put an end to the disagreement. I asked myself, 'Is teaching something I really want to do for the rest of my life?'

As the weeks went by, the Grade 9s became more manageable. They weren't the best-behaved class, by any standard, but for their class they were becoming well behaved. As I began taking on more responsibilities in the Grade 10 art class and with the Grade 9 social science class, I also volunteered to coach the school field hockey team. Although this added extra time and work to my school responsibilities, it was one of my most satisfying experiences at the school. I had a really great group of girls who came out to practice and tried to improve their skills. It was a relaxing way to complete a day of school, especially when I was stressed from trying to teach the Grade 9 students. We had a lot of fun during practices and they had fun playing during the games. It was a time when I did not have to worry about arguments and I could just make up drills off the top of my head. We finished in ninth place and missed the quarter-finals, but I had achieved my main goals of teaching them how to play hockey and having fun.

In my first eight weeks of teaching, I learned many lessons, although I still have many more to learn. Don't expect all the students in your class to like you; you should expect them to respect you. Be open, friendly and caring. Treat all students with respect. It's up to them if they keep it or lose it! I was told that I shouldn't smile until Christmas, but I think that as long as you are firm and consistent with classroom rules you can get away with smiling on your second day! As teacher candidates and beginning teachers, it is important that we find our own teaching styles and not copy other teachers. Not only do we cheat ourselves, we also shortchange our students. However, we can try different techniques from other teachers and incorporate their styles and ideas into our own. Give students a chance to prove themselves and make your own decisions about them, their behaviour and their achievement before you consult their school records. Teach them to treat themselves and each other with respect. Try out your lessons and assignments first, so that you can help the students around some of their frustrations. It is also a good idea to let the students see that you are human and that you do make mistakes. *Don't ever be afraid to apologize.*

You will never stop being a student of learning. There are almost always more well-behaved students than misbehaving ones. Removing only two students from the class can make an incredible difference! Stand up for yourself and the other students; don't let the one or two misbehaving students ruin it for the rest of the class. Know your limits, and don't let the students push you over the edge. Give students a second chance to improve themselves. Above all, look for rewards and improvements, no matter how small. I was able to have one student who never took notes or did homework copy a complete note from the board. Another student whose reading skills seemed very limited began to answer questions on his own instead of copying answers from his neighbour. He not only completed an essay, but he also handed it in on time!

Don't be afraid to be friendly with your students. You don't need to become friends; just have friendly conversations and get to know them on an individual basis. There are several students in the three classes I have been working with whom I am getting to know very well just through short conversations regarding school and general interests. In the Grade 10 art class, I have one student who likes to tell me to 'get lost' with a great big smile on his face when I've given him too many suggestions for his art works.

I hope that you don't get the feeling I think that teaching will be a bed of roses. If you do end up with a great class, treasure the experience! However, don't become frustrated if you do have a difficult class. During my eighth week with the Grade 9 students I was working with a supply teacher. After the second day together she wondered if I worried about having to face the Grade 9 class every day. Since I am an eternal optimist, I replied that I looked forward to the challenge of having them behave and learn something each day. Sometimes, this learning can consist of finally being able to do something by themselves. Out of the three classes that I have been working with, my most rewarding class has been the Grade 9. I have had to break up confrontations, I was stuck in the middle of a very tense situation, and I have had to deal with many behaviour problems, yet they have grown so much in the last eight weeks! During my first week back at the Faculty of Education, I popped into both my Grade 10 art class and my Grade 9 social science class and discovered that they really did miss me and valued having me in their classrooms. I'm looking forward to my next six weeks with all of the students I have come to know since September and I know I will miss them greatly at the end of December.

Teaching is worth all of the blood, sweat and tears in the end, when you see one of the hardest-to-reach students dressed as a woman for Hallowe'en (make-up, nylons, hat and dress!) who yells out 'I love you, Ms. Berndt!' as you leave the class when you've only been absent for four days!

Rare, Beautiful Moments
Christina Morgan

Teaching as a teacher candidate for an extended period of time has pushed my mind and body in many different ways. Every day forces me to question my beliefs concerning education. My experiences have pulled back the curtains to reveal a world that was previously unfamiliar to me — a world where the 'right' thing does not always happen and where policy clashes with reality. Working in a school has allowed me to see the 'reality' of an environment where students' needs are met to the best of the staff's ability. Unfortunately, the process is not always adequate because there are not enough resources to satisfy the school's requirements. Students' needs are prioritized; those whose needs are seen as lowest are often left without any assistance.

Yet the world in which my teaching experience has unfolded is not entirely negative; it includes the magic that exists within the four walls of a classroom. For a brief moment, magic can emerge when small hands fly upwards, eyes open wide, and bodies inch forward. A new realm opens, created by the potential of the students. Labels disappear and all that exists is the freedom to learn. These are rare, beautiful moments. I do not continually search for them. Appreciating what occurs in between is equally important as this time is a valuable part of the journey. Often, in teaching, 'apparent' failures can miraculously become successes in the classroom. It is my observation of, and participation in, this learning journey that have made my recent teaching experiences rich and colourful. These experiences have been, and continue to be, difficult and heartbreaking. However, they have given me an opportunity to search within myself and question why I have chosen to teach.

I continually ask myself, 'What do I hope to accomplish?' and 'Can I make a difference?' While searching for answers, I continue to develop a strong passion for teaching that gives me strength to pursue my goals and to continue to redefine them. My experiences have further developed my understanding of what teaching entails, and I have come to accept that sometimes the right answer can be impossible to find. In my experience, while trying to uncover the voices of my students, I have started to find my own individual voice. It is this discovery that has given me the confidence, authority and strength to continue to follow my goal of providing a safe, comfortable, healthy space for learning.

Teaching is a Work-in-Progress
Virgenia Aquino Yee

I am the middle child of a mother who immigrated from Manila, Philippines, and a father who immigrated from Canton, China. I was born and raised in Cornwall, Ontario, which is quite near to the Quebec, Cornwall Island and New York State borders. In this account I offer reflections on myself as a beginning teacher and, where appropriate, on my life story.

From as early as the age of 4, I remember having to form a concept of myself. As a young child growing up, I was surrounded by caring relatives of my father's family but I still did not really find myself identifying with either of my parents' cultural heritages. I grew up in, and still reside in, a French–Canadian neighborhood. Because my parents spoke English 'differently,' and because we, as a family, did many things 'differently,' my perception of life was that of a social and cultural outsider looking in. My parents attempted to raise me by strict Asian traditions. They encouraged me to embrace their heritage and the culture in which I live. At times I celebrated this uniqueness and at other times I felt overwhelmed by the marked scrutiny. Over the years, I remember having to explain and teach ideas to different people. In doing this I questioned what happens during my own learning process and came to regularly ask how I reached the point where I found myself. In my years as a student, I remember the teachers who encouraged me not only to be myself but to also be a critical thinker. I would describe myself as a person who approaches life as an explorer of ideas. I believe that my friends, my parents and the teacher who came into my life have all helped to shape the way that I teach students in the classroom and at the school.

These first nine weeks of teaching have made me realize that I have changed. I am no longer the teacher-person I was even a month ago. I am still changing with every new experience. I am figuring out who Virgenia Yee, the teacher, really is. As a newcomer to this 'lifestyle of the teacher,' I have been struggling to form my identity as a teacher. Looking back over my years as a student, I recall the influential teachers of my life. The turning point in my years as a student occurred at age 9 in Grade 4. For the first time, my grades were no longer compared to my older sister's, and I was encouraged to be myself, to be Virgenia! Mr Andrews was an inspirational teacher, and although he passed away only two years after I met him, the way he taught remains with me to this day. He worked hard to capture my curiosity and interest during his class. There were also days when he proved himself to be not only a remarkable teacher but also a sincere human being. In high school, my English teachers, Mr Blackadder and Mrs Hill, encouraged me to write poetry and to express my thoughts. These teachers instilled in me a sense of pride in my own work and in myself as the author.

The best part of my several short teaching placements during my undergraduate years in the Concurrent Education Program at Queen's University was the rapport I developed with my associate teachers in Cornwall, Kingston and Scarborough. The placements were so short that there was little time to discuss the issues and concerns that arose in my mind and, although I treasured these experiences, I now see them as 'artificial.' Since late August, when I entered the Pilot Program in the Faculty of Education, my life as a teacher has been much less artificial. It is an incredible experience: here I am, in front of the class, at the school, planning, teaching and contributing to my associate school's community. Although this practicum has been overwhelming, I have discovered that I really do want to be a teacher!

My life as a 'teacher' began when I attended the first staff meeting of the school year last August, a few days before the school year began. To date, I have been to the staff meetings, the department meetings, PA days, Parent–Teacher Interviews, meetings with the student counselors, and school assemblies. I am even helping my associate teachers present an after-school 'Scope and Sequence' workshop for other teachers and principals. In the remaining two months of this placement, I will be working with the school council to revise the Safe Schools Policy and the Student Code of Behaviour; conducting a relaxation exercise for at-risk students in an anger-management group; advising the school's

Improvisation Team; and working with the students and drama teachers on a Children's Theatre play and on the school play to be presented in the Spring. This pilot program has given me many opportunities to talk to teachers about their work and about my own work and my professional development. It is this forming of relationships with the students and the teachers that enticed me to become a part of this program. I now realize that teaching is a passion that I have to keep working at.

The first day of school was both frightening and exciting. I was frightened, in the sense that I had so many new decisions to make: minute details became critical, from what I would eat for breakfast to remembering my map of the school. I was excited by the fact that this time I was beginning school on the very first day, and this time as a teacher! I was a bit nervous in learning all the names not only of the students but also of the staff. I was really looking forward to meeting new people and teaching the subjects I love — Drama and English! It was on that first day that I had to 'take inventory of my identity,' in order to give some interesting facts about myself and introduce myself as 'Miss Yee.' I had to find my voice and develop a presence as a teacher.

Organization and advance notice are paramount to a teacher candidate's smooth transition into a school. We had an intensive and stressful orientation week at the Faculty, and my beginning days at the school seemed rocky at first. I had no idea who my associate teachers from the English department would be. The fact that the vice-principal formally introduced and welcomed me at that first staff meeting in August made a world of difference. The vice-principal ensured that all the staff knew who the Pilot Program candidates were; he also pointed out that we were not going to be at their school for just a couple of weeks. We were committed to being a part of the school community from September to December, and to returning for another placement in May.

One of my associate teachers remarked that it takes a lot of courage to participate in such a demanding program. In this Pilot Program, each teacher candidate has field-based course work added onto the teaching load and the extracurricular involvement. An associate teacher also stressed that the Faculty of Education really needed to revamp its program, and I have to agree. I have one friend in the regular program who often finds herself bored. In this Pilot Program we are asked to teach every day and keep up with the demands of several experience-based education courses. At times, these demands are overwhelming. What this program asks one to do is to take risks and adapt to the lifestyle of teaching. I had to cope with the new changes in my identity and role as a teacher, familiarize myself with the school, learn the new bus route to school, adapt to the school's new time schedule, and move into a new apartment. I have gained some insight into the routine of life at school as a beginning teacher. You won't get very much sleep because there is so much work to do in creating interesting and flexible lessons. Your social life comes to a standstill. There is a lot to keep track of in terms of paperwork and students' behaviour, and about how each student learns. You should understand the expectations of your program thoroughly beforehand, and you will, because the people around you will ask you about it.

On reflection, there are a few important concepts that I want to incorporate into my teaching. The first is that each student should be comfortable with understanding how he or she arrived at an answer. I don't want students to repeat the exact information on their papers; I want them to call their work their own. The second concept that I want to strive for is that I structure my teaching so that my lessons are relevant to the lives of these students. I hope they make the unfamiliar familiar. The third concept is that the students feel safe and secure in themselves to express their ideas in my classroom, and the fourth is that I hope to instill in my students the importance of drama, the languages, and all arts, and to encourage them to incorporate all of these into their lives.

At this point in my internship I have been asking different teachers many questions about their experiences and their own practices in teaching, and they have related to me, in turn, their different methods of approaching particular problems. I have made invaluable contacts with people at my school and at other schools that I am certain I would not have made if I had only been at this school for a placement of three weeks.

I am striving to teach the students to the best of my abilities, and hoping to convey a sense of humanity to them. I am working on being flexible in my lessons and on anticipating when to 'shift gears' in my teaching for the different levels of learners and the variety of personalities in the class. My action research project will focus on asking better questions. My voice has improved from when I first started teaching, and I am becoming more comfortable with pausing and learning to redirect my questions. I am still searching for and building my resources for teaching. I try to emphasize accountability to the students, so that they are responsible for the choices they make in their learning and in the directions they choose. In my practice I attempt to instill in the students my respect for their responses to my teaching, and the importance of my own and their responses to my teaching of the other students in the class.

As a new teacher with much more to learn, I have discovered how essential it is that I realize that teaching through a lesson plan is not as important as *remembering that I am teaching people*. I have experienced those special teaching moments when the students and I were so interested and absorbed in our work that the period just flew by. There have also been other days when the lessons just did not work for the students. In my experiences so far, I have found that teaching demands thoughtful planning, imagination, creativity, compromise, and discipline. It asks that you examine how your feelings about certain issues will affect your personal and professional responses to people. I am discovering who I am as a teacher person, what my teaching style is, and what my responsibilities and roles are as a professional. In this process I am making connections with people and gaining insights from their experiences. I have a need to teach — teaching is a personal passion. My development as a teacher is an ongoing, lifelong learning process. The first eight weeks have given me the confidence to say, 'Yes, this is a lot of work, but with others to guide me I can work this through.' If I can somehow understand where the students are coming from in life, I hope that they in turn can relate to where I am going with my teaching.

Prepare Yourself
Angela Tung

Prepare yourself for joining the ranks of coffee worshippers and thinking that the world has come to an end when the office runs out of milk and sugar.

Prepare yourself for late nights preparing lessons and racking your brain for exciting and motivating ideas.

In the mornings, expect pasty-mouth and sleep-crusty eyes and wondering why you're doing this to yourself.

Prepare for 100m dashes to the photocopier and frantic line-ups as you wait to make that last minute set of handouts for the class that has just begun.

But remember the comforting feeling you will get when you have the next three days planned out as you watch your colleagues scramble around like headless chickens.

Prepare for row upon row of young faces — some eager, some indifferent, some asleep.

Expect the pulse-racing, palm-sweating moments when you question whether the demonstration you're about to do will actually work.

Be ready (if teaching science) for such unforeseen incidents as exploding crucibles, chemical fires and smelly beans (don't ask).

Prepare yourself for the cries of 'Oh neat!', 'That's so cool,' and 'I finally get it!' and know that you've done your job.

Prepare for the elation when you reach the one student who 'hates' your subject.

Remember when they compliment you on your handwriting; it's the only way for them to say 'I like you' without seeming uncool.

Expect those days when *nothing* goes right, and know that it's not all your fault.

Prepare for the next day, when everything does go right and you think 'I'm not so bad after all.'

Most of all, prepare for your students, and remember that you hold part of their future in your hands.

Chapter 6

Sink or Swim? — Voices of Extended Experience

Members of the 1996 Queen's–Waterloo Science Group

Overview

The series of short entries in this chapter gives a sense of what it is like to be immersed in four months of teaching after one week of orientation. While most programs of pre-service teacher education provide a more gradual introduction to a full-time experience of teaching, there always comes a time when it is 'now or never.' The first time one stands before an entire class, knowing that many more lessons will follow, is a unique moment for each of us entering the teaching profession. In that sense, we hope that the voices presented here will be helpful to every new teacher about to 'take the plunge.' These entries were written at the start of a four-month term of education courses, immediately after four months of teaching, and these questions were posed to help people find an initial sense of voice:

> Was it 'sink or swim'? Did you feel like you were sinking? How soon did you feel like you were swimming instead? What role did the teachers in the school have in your 'learning to swim'?

Impressions of Learning by Early Experience

Nicole
My first few weeks were terrible! Well, I thought that they were terrible. My biggest problem initially was speaking in front of a class. I was very nervous. My associate teacher reassured me that I was doing well, but I felt that I was doing a lousy job! However, one day after class I was talking to a student about how he liked the class. I asked him how he thought I was doing as a teacher. He thought I was doing just fine. He didn't seem to notice (or at least he didn't tell me) when

I made a mistake or when I rambled on and on during the class. Maybe he was just being polite when he said these things, but it did wonders for my confidence! Although I had the support of my associate teacher and other teachers in the school, it wasn't until this student commented on my work that I felt like I was 'swimming.' Even if he didn't really mean what he said, I guess he saved me from 'sinking.'

Another concern I had about going into the classroom was that the students wouldn't think of me a teacher. Going back to my high school only three years after graduation, as a teacher, might feel strange, I thought. However, the teachers in my high school (well, most of them) treated me like one of their colleagues and the students also treated and respected me like a teacher. Overall, the experience was not 'sink or swim' but rather 'learning to swim.'

* * * * *

Dustin

I had few problems. Most of my associates had me observe at the first of the year in order to allow me to get used to the class, etc. They gave me more responsibility until finally I had control of my classes. My associates were quick to give advice and, what I needed to know, I soon picked up. I did not feel really comfortable, though, until the last few weeks of the term. I think that this was because it took me that long to feel confident in what I was doing. The class noticed this, and I think that they must know that the teacher feels confident before they can feel comfortable with the situation.

I think that going into the practice teaching experience without any preconceived ideas is helpful, too. I found that it helped me develop a style based on what worked for me, rather than what theory told me I should do. Now, the theory should be more meaningful and easier to implement in useful ways which will improve my skills.

* * * * *

Andrea

I'm not sure that any amount of preparation will relieve you of those first day jitters. The part I found most frustrating was the lack of knowledge of 'education lingo.' It's hard to communicate when you don't know how to say what you want to ask. The associate directs you in words and phrases you haven't heard before: OHP, teaching methods, kinaesthetic learners or unit aims. It's English, but not really part of your understanding.

I know now of many books that I'll be reading, questions I need to ask, and things I need to learn, but it wasn't until I had been teaching for a week before I really knew what to ask or where I needed help. In this way, 'the sink or swim' method is excellent. You find the questions you need to ask because they are personally relevant: 'I need to know this to survive!' Before I had done some teaching I had *no* idea of where I needed help. Afterwards I had a list of questions as long as my arm.

At times I felt like I was sinking, but who doesn't? I found experienced teachers also felt at times like they were sinking, too. I had an excellent associate who was able to put out the 'life preserver' for me, and I was soon feeling more secure. It wasn't very long before I was swimming again. However, I don't really feel that it was a case of sinking and then I was swimming; it was more an up-and-down situation — I would swim, and then sink, and swim again.

The teachers at the school were fabulous. They were continually putting things in my box, adding suggestions, helping out, encouraging me, and being there when I needed it. They had everything to do with teaching me how to swim. Perhaps this is not the easiest way to dive into teaching, but it really makes the learning curve increase exponentially! I wouldn't do it any other way.

* * * * *

Stacey
That first day — a bundle of nerves, very unsure of what was going to happen, I did not feel that I sunk or swam — the best description is 'treading water.' When I was thrown in the first day, and introduced as a 'teacher,' I was quite unsure of myself, especially the approach that I would take to teach the students. My associates were wonderful; I gradually learned how to swim. By mid-October I was extremely comfortable with myself as well as with my students. From that period forward I was swimming laps — extremely confident in developing my own *teaching* style.

This program's experience is *wonderful.* I believe that I have learned a lot already without any formal training. I believe it is shocking at first, but eventually you will begin to feel like a teacher! At first you are quite uncomfortable — nervous, maybe even slightly scared. You tread water for a while. Then eventually you learn to swim. That was my experience. My associates were good role models. One of my associates had quite a different approach to teaching from what I would use. This was a learning experience because at first it was hard to model the teacher — I was not my associate, and had to soon develop a style of teaching distinct from his. Although the teaching styles were different, I was continually encouraged. Support from all staff was wonderful.

This program is the best way to experience real 'teaching.' I believe that you cannot grasp a true teaching style by practicing to teach for only a few weeks at time. Four months is more practical. In this time you get to know your students and watch their development throughout the term. By this I mean you can see the trends — what comes easily and what was hard material for the class — lessons — how to plan for a specific class — what will catch their attention. In four months you can really get a 'sense' of teaching. It was a wonderful experience, when you look back on it; at the time it was scary at first. Eventually, with support from my associates as well as other staff members, I learned to swim.

* * * * *

Peter

I do think that it is a sink-or-swim experience, but in a wading pool. By this I mean it is very difficult to sink, due to the support from staff. I simply watched classes for the first couple of weeks, and made many observations and did a lot of thinking, and then gave it a try. The first couple of days there was a lot of consultation with my associate, but then I knew what was expected and what I expected from myself, and set out to experiment. I think the associate plays an enormous role for the first month, and this could be a weak point to the program if an associate teacher is not very good at this role. I was fortunate to have an excellent associate teacher who fed me countless stories and worked with (massaged) my ideas, but let me make my own mistakes and gain my own victories.

I think that another important element and possible weak point is the willingness of the student to do work for other teachers. I found that marking tests or assignments and helping with lab preps or actual labs with *anybody* was very valuable. I was exposed in this way to many different styles and attitudes which, for the most part, gave me more confidence because I could see certain elements about other teachers that I preferred to my style or attitude to theirs. I think these two elements, the associate and the attitude of the student, are two critical elements to the experience, and to whether you sink or swim.

* * * * *

Patricia

It was definitely swimming. I believe that in the kind of job I had [as a supply teacher], you have to be responsible, that is, learn to adapt to the situation you are in. At first I was very nervous going into a classroom, but I learned to cope with this kind of feeling. I received a lot of help from the vice-principal; he was my mentor. He guided me and gave me some input into what I should do, but he also left the last word to me. It was up to me to decide how to handle a situation. It took me about a month to feel completely secure in what I was doing. There were some situations I did not know how to handle, or students' reactions that made me want to throw in the towel. Giving it all up would be the easy way out, and I believe perseverance is the key for everything. I also had a great associate teacher; he gave me input in the lessons I did, as well as advice in certain situations so that I could improve. I believe the hardest part of teaching is classroom management. As a teacher, I had to find ways to handle these situations. Participating in extra-curricular activities gave me the chance to get to know some students and for them to get to know me. I have also learned to be flexible in the way I approach students. I still have to work more on this one, though.

* * * * *

Colin

I think that Derek's book [an early draft of this collection] says it all: 'No one can tell you how to teach, you learn from experience.' Granted, the past four months were a 'trial by fire,' but I learned so much! Since I was there for four months, my associates slowly introduced me into the course. During the first week, I observed and I helped with homework and labs. It wasn't until the end of the second week that I taught my first class, and then it slowly picked up from there.

My survival was a lot of instinct. I believe that a lot of teaching is done by instinct, and developed by past experiences. Although I don't have many personal teaching experiences, I have been a student for many years! I just adopted the things that my teachers used with me, and worked them into different situations. The staff at my school were extremely supportive, and they tried to understand my situation. Advice was plentiful, and they definitely helped in the early weeks. After that, a lot of my learning about teaching was supervised trial and error! The best way to learn!

* * * * *

Ray

It turned out for me that it really wasn't as difficult as I thought it would be. Of course, you don't start out teaching the class immediately, and after a few days you get a good feeling of what the students are like. The first time I taught them I'd say was a 'swim' or, at least, a 'float.' As the term progressed, I had a few days where I was sinking no matter what I did. Each of those sinking days was a learning experience; the 'mistakes' I made I'll never make again. Practice teaching is the time to make those mistakes because you are still developing your style.

The associate teachers can make a big difference in what you get out of your practice teaching. I found that most of the time the associate teacher is very supportive and tolerant of your inexperience. At times you may feel that he or she is not giving you enough flexibility or responsibility for what you are teaching, but in any job you don't get to start at the top.

* * * * *

Melanie

I was excited about teaching in a high school for the first time, but when I heard about having entire classes to myself I was scared. I didn't feel I knew enough to teach. The trick is, you don't need to *know* it, you just need to be able to familiarize yourself with the material before you present it. I worked in outdoor education, and programs changed from week to week. The hours were long, so there was no real chance to explore ahead of time. Sometimes I *sank*, and begged off a program I was unsure of. Mostly I swam by taking an unfamiliar program if other staff were unable to teach.

Learning to swim was just becoming familiar enough with your surroundings to feel comfortable about doing anything. You had to risk trouble, in a way, to learn what you could/should do. But, hey! these are the times to make mistakes! Having associates who encouraged 'Do it your way' programming enabled me to begin to develop a style as opposed to just following instructions. Hey, if you are scared, it means you want to do well. Hence, you had better be scared?

* * * * *

Steph

Sinking, swimming . . . it's all relative. How long can you hold your breath? Starting off the term teaching, with nothing much more than a shove off the edge of the pool, was definitely a challenge. But, as in all things, you will learn. Starting off, first plug your nose and thrash about, hoping to get a gulp of air once in a while. Learning to swim on your own is difficult. So is learning to teach on your own. However, you eventually get the rhythm, the style that best suits you, and that you feel most comfortable with. Having already tried teaching, I will now be more responsive to the coaching received from the profs at Queen's.

The key is wanting to learn, and being ready to take risks — and enjoying or suffering the consequences, whatever they may be. Students are generally candid, and they will let you know soon enough how you are doing. A few weeks into the term, I was swimming comfortably; however, throughout the term, I got some cramps and started sinking again (or at least bobbing up and down). I believe that all of teaching is a continuous struggle. If you stop doing the front crawl and start doing the dead man's float — coasting alone — the sinking will start all over.

Overall, I think the experience was great. I didn't just get my feet wet, I got drenched! But it was worth it. The best way to learn something is to get right into it. After all, a duckling would never learn to swim, or an eagle would never learn to fly, without that first dive into the pond or the first nudge out of the nest.

* * * * *

Laurie

It's pretty strange, but I actually felt like I was swimming my first days of teaching. I slowly started to sink soon after because I started to see the problems that could arise; however, although I asked for advice on how to handle them, I mainly dealt with them my own way. The major sinking feeling came from the workload. I realize now that I maybe gave too many tests, labs and assignments. If I were to do it again, I'd probably cut down on the marking about 20 per cent.

My associate teachers really didn't help me that much in terms of lesson plans and tests. They never helped me mark papers because they wanted me to get a true feel for the teaching profession. Most of my questions dealt with discipline and only occasionally did I ask for help on lesson plan materials. I never really felt like it was 'sink-or-swim' because my associate teachers were almost always in the room. They almost never contributed to my classes but I always felt like they would handle any major problems. Thank goodness they didn't have to.

* * * * *

Kate

Well, for me, I wasn't at a 'school,' but an outdoor education centre. Since I worked there my previous work term, I was one of the only staff members who knew how things ran. I really enjoyed teaching the new staff the 'ins and outs' of D_____ Forest. The facilitator of the centre was a great help in allowing me to do most of the staff training. I think that I did a good job in showing the staff how most of the programs were normally taught, but also in letting them know that they could teach how they wanted.

Teaching for me this term was fun and exciting, but not really new. Sure, I changed my methods and learned through experience how to do them better, but the type of teaching that I experienced wasn't really new. I hope that the experience I have gained from teaching outdoor education so long will allow me to contribute as much as anyone else. Teaching inside a 'real' classroom will still be a first experience for me when we head out on our practicum. I'm looking forward to interacting with the older students and teachers inside a school. But, for now, I hope to learn from my friends here, and hear of their experiences and put in my views as best I can. Responding to the last question, I have found that all teachers have been helpful in answering my questions and giving me some feedback on my lessons and programs.

* * * * *

Margaret

The first part of my teaching placement was spent at _____ Out-door Education Centre. During my first few days I had some feelings of doubt, but my associate teacher was great. He informed me that 'we,' the staff, were all teachers and we were all equal. This put my mind at ease, as I was no longer the low person on the totem pole. I was equal. My associate's easy-going attitude allowed me to feel comfortable about teaching and experimenting with my lessons.

The second part of my teaching placement was spent at _____ Secondary School. This is where I started to sink. I went from swimming to sinking in a matter of two days. I think the fact that I had been removed from a high school setting so long made me feel uncomfortable in the classroom. I don't know if the kids could feel that I was uncomfortable; they didn't treat me like a teacher or an 'equal teacher.' They treated me like a supply or student teacher, and I guess that is what I was. However, I had spent the last two months as an equal, and I was not used to being called a 'student teacher.' My associate could tell after my first week that I wasn't accustomed to the 'traditional' classroom setting and gave me some advice that helped a lot. From this point forward, things changed for the better every day!

* * * * *

Kevin

I didn't feel that I was sinking too much. Without the orientation in August I would have been pretty lost, but I found that week to be very helpful. I always felt that if I needed to I could refer to some of the material that was handed out, or I could contact other QW [Queen's–Waterloo] students through e-mail. It was good to feel that I was really learning to teach, and without too much pressure to 'prove myself.' The teachers I worked with were great; they gave me lots of advice and were pretty supportive of me trying new things in the class that were a bit different from their approach. My general attitude was that I was training to be a teacher, and that there was lots to learn. If I was great at some things in the class, that was great. Finding out some of my weaknesses enables me to really focus on them now, while at the Faculty of Education. The other thing that really helped was that I observed the classes on the first few days before having to start teaching.

* * * * *

Anne

I started my teaching placement the day after Labour Day. I got there at 8 am and followed my associate around until lunch. On the way to the cafeteria he asked what class I would be most interested in teaching; I told him Grade 11 biology. In the cafeteria, he introduced me to a very enthusiastic Grade 11 biology teacher, and asked if I could work with her. She said, 'Yes,' and they both recommended I start *that day*! They felt that way the class would be mine. I politely said I'd like to wait a bit, maybe observe for a while. I did, however, set up labs, help with labs, and start marking right away. In the first few weeks I really felt like I was sinking, and a few times I questioned if teaching was for me. On September 25th I began teaching. The teacher said, 'Good luck!' and shut the door on the way out. The first week or two, teaching *was* really overwhelming. Teachers were supportive by helping me plan, and offering advice.

After the first couple of weeks, something clicked: I was 'Miss S_____.' I walked down the hall, and students shouted, 'Hi, Miss S_____!' and students were now coming to me for help! So it was 'sink or swim!' I managed to survive! I'm glad that I had to work so hard. It made me realize that I wanted to teach, and it was worth it!

* * * * *

Heidi

I must admit that my thoughts at the beginning of September were of panic. Soon after being exposed to the teaching experience, everything fell into place. I never really felt as though I were sinking. There were times and days that I came close, but my associate teachers were amazing.

I found that a lot of the teachers at my school were unfamiliar with the QW [Queen's–Waterloo] program. I spent a fair bit of time explaining it. Everyone, including me, thought it was a great idea to teach first before arriving here. You can't really teach someone how to teach; you can only guide them. Therefore, by having four months of practical experience, I feel I will benefit more during my time here at Queen's than other students (not QW). I have experiences, both good and bad, and I can improve through my learning here. I know what didn't work, and hopefully will gain some knowledge at Queen's to improve or modify situations. I'm not coming into teacher's college blind; I've taught, and I know the basics. Now I'm ready to learn how to make what I know better — more dynamic. Maybe the reason I'm so positive about this set-up is because my associates did give me a lot of guidance. First of all, it helps to work with those same teachers that you looked up to and respected during your high school years. I started teaching my Grade 9 and Grade 11 class from day one — I was their teacher. People couldn't believe that I was in this situation without any formal instruction. My associates felt it was the best way to learn. This way the students would see me, not my associate, as their teacher. My associates never left me to sink. They helped me with techniques that I felt comfortable with, and guided me through rough situations. I had an amazing experience which makes me very confident that I will be a teacher one day. The last four months also left me very excited to come to Queen's and to learn more.

* * * * *

Laura

In the beginning, I felt that going out to teach before teacher's college was a little backwards. In the end, however, I felt that it turned out to be a good thing. I was a little nervous and unsure at the beginning, but after a week or two I felt much more comfortable. While teaching, I quickly discovered my strengths and weaknesses. I feel that my teaching experience will help me get more out of my time here. Sharing and learning from others will be very useful.

My two associate teachers and fellow co-op students were great. They were so enthusiastic and full of great ideas. The teachers always gave positive feedback and also many good suggestions. Many resources were available to plan our lessons. Seeing the way different teachers dealt with problems allowed me to see how students reacted to different forms of discipline. I was able to discover the method which worked best for me.

In the beginning I felt like I was sinking when it came to discipline, but I quickly came to realize that it was more important for the kids to respect me, rather than just like me. After a few weeks I gained better control. The teachers I worked with gave me independence and respect as a teacher. They quickly helped me to swim in a field in which it is so easy to sink.

* * * * *

Shelly

The first week of school in September I was teaching OAC chemistry by the Friday of that week. For the rest of the first week I was observing several classes and was itching to start into something. The first time I stepped in front of the eager faces of thirty students, my stomach dropped out of my body, and I thought it was all over. The lesson went all right, but I wasn't completely satisfied. It wasn't until about the second week or so of teaching that I started to feel comfortable. Subsequently, when I took on a Grade 10 class, I started to feel a little too busy. I can say that, from the point where I was prepping for more than one class, I constantly felt I was sinking. I think that there was only one time in my entire four months of teaching when I felt completely on top of things. The rest of the time it felt as though things were on top of me!

For me, it was definitely a sink-or-swim issue at first. For a while I was swimming, but for the most part I was treading water and just keeping my head above the surface. My one associate was a great help in lending an ear and offering suggestions for my many dilemmas, but the other seemed to think I should be able to think through them myself and ultimately *know* how to get through them on my own.

* * * * *

Stephanie

It was a sink-or-swim experience, but my associates were so helpful that it was very easy to swim. The first few days were confusing because I was a little unsure what my role in the classroom was while I was just observing. After the first week, I was slowly starting to supervise labs and do some teaching and, as soon as I did that, I felt that I fitted right in. My first lessons always flew by, but I never seemed to be able to stick to the lesson plan. It took me a few days to figure out how fast to move, and what the class could cover. My associates were helpful because they gave some advice but basic-ally let me find my own pace and style of teaching. When I was worried about my classes taking too long, they told me that this often happens, even to experienced teachers. Surviving the term with so little background wasn't difficult because my associates gave me the freedom to try things when I felt ready to do them, so I always felt prepared.

The Voice of a Poet Learning to Teach, 3

Tanya Marwitz

Human Potential

'What are you talking about . . .'
'Oh, now I get it . . .'
'Do you mean like this . . .'
'What about you ?'
'Yeah, but I had one . . .'
'My mommy said . . .'
'. . . and then there was one that . . .'
'Hey, me too!'

Their questions are endless, their comments refreshing,
their knowledge runs deeper than I credit them for.
They build from perspectives I've forgotten I had
and scribble for reasons I hadn't explored.

Thirty-eight eyes see things I can't find
and are acutely aware of one teacher's faults.
Nineteen minds offer ideas unheard of
as I try to find keys to their imaginations' vaults.

Though some of their movements may appear awkward,
they always draw big what they like best.
Their quest for truth is never-ending
and their need for justice is always expressed.

They love,
they inspire,
they learn
and they'll lead
and their human potential
is all this world needs.

(September 1996 — from observations of the
5- and 6-year-olds in my first class)

Chapter 7

Learning to Teach:
A Story of Five Crises

Kevin Smith

Overview

This account of nine months focused on learning to teach caught our attention because Kevin casts it so clearly in terms of 'crises' that represented challenges to his assumptions about what learning to teach should involve. The story is written informally, and we believe it is best left in its original form. At times, Kevin's account may appear 'unprofessional' when he is critical of the teachers who took him into their classrooms for four months. We believe Kevin is very honest about his feelings during his first four months of teaching, when he was largely on his own to make sense of what was happening to him, and we believe that many new teachers experience similar initial re-actions to experienced teachers' classroom practices. As noted else-where, learning to teach, like teaching itself, is a uniquely personal experience. We are grateful to Kevin for permission to include his story in this collection.

A Story of Five Crises

I seem to have had five big crises as I learned to teach. After each crisis, my views and attitudes concerning teaching underwent a major over-haul. The first crisis came after the first week of orientation in August. The second occurred after the first four months of teaching (September to December), while the third occurred after those initial weeks (Janu-ary) spent here at Queen's. After three more weeks of teaching (Feb-ruary), I had another big switch of attitudes. Finally, during my last few weeks of classes at Queen's (March and April), I didn't experience any crises at all, and that may be a crisis as well!

August Orientation Week

Back in August I wasn't sure what teaching was going to be all about. I remember that my greatest concern was classroom management. What would I do if I couldn't get the kids to pay attention and behave? As that week of orientation began, that was the topic I really wanted to cover. I wanted to hear disciplinary stories — successes and failures — people's opinions on the subject of classroom management, and most of all I hoped to get a few strategies on maintaining discipline in the class. I remember not being too worried about making science interesting (I guess I was one of the fortunate kids in that I had pretty much always found it interesting myself in high school regardless of the teacher); I also didn't worry about cool demos (I think I thought my associate could help with those), or marking, or lab safety (I worried about law suits a little, but I thought I'd make out OK overall), or many of the other issues that we all wanted to cover that week in August. I think the only other issue that worried me was how would I be able to *entertain* the kids for 75 minutes, but by far my worst worry was classroom management.

Before orientation began in August I thought that we'd be having 'real' classes during that week. I was hoping to have some serious lectures on classroom management. Now that seems totally absurd, but at the time I thought that that was the way to learn. I enjoyed hearing about the experiences of the guys who had made it through Queen's, but I thought that real learning would occur once we got down to listening to someone talk about classroom management *to* us.

By the end of that week I thought the only thing I'd accomplished was getting a little familiar with everyone's face in the group (by January I had forgotten almost everyone's again). Actually I also knew some of the key elements to include in a lesson plan (I used them for the first four or five lesson plans I made, maybe), and I felt happy that at least we'd discussed classroom management. I was excited to get to the school I'd be teaching at. I wanted to get a class of my own. I wanted to get to know some kids. I wanted to make a difference. I don't think I felt empowered to do so, but I was anxious for the chance to try out this whole teaching thing. And that was the first turning point in my attitude towards teaching. Before that week in August, I was thinking that teaching would be OK, that I'd get along great with the kids, but that I wanted to attend some formal lectures on methods of teaching and learning. I wanted to get a bit of a structured education where someone would thrust the information at me. With those tools I thought I'd be pretty well able to get out and teach. At the end of that week,

I'd had enough of talking about teaching. I didn't know what I'd do in a lot of the situations we'd discussed that week (what if a kid started acting up, or threatened me, or started fighting with another kid?). I was anxious to get my feet wet. I still felt like I didn't know too much. I was still concerned about classroom management, but I wanted to get some real world experience.

Before that week in August, I wanted to learn lots and lots about the theory of teaching. I think I thought there was some kind of textbook I could just read to find out all I needed to know about teaching. I knew that there could be wide variation among teaching styles, but I thought that a couple of well-thought out texts could encompass all that. After that week, I still thought that I had a lot to learn about the theory of teaching (like everything), but I felt that I needed to get a handle on the practical side of things.

Crisis 1 — Someone forgot to give me the instruction manual on teaching.

Real Teaching for Four Months (September to December)

Then came my first placement — for four months! At first I couldn't believe the responsibilities that I was given when I waltzed into N____ Collegiate Institute (NCI — a placement I found myself!). I had met my associate before and I decided on NCI based on the recommendations of some of my friends. Looking back I have more and more mixed feelings about the whole experience as time goes by, but at the time I thought the school was pretty cool. I was excited. Then I met the kids. And I was still excited! They were great. I also felt like I was fairly privileged; it was a thrill just to go in the staff room the first time! It was like looking at the inner-workings of a machine I'd been around my whole life but that I was never allowed to understand. Weird analogy but I think it's appropriate. Getting back to the responsibilities, I got to start marking immediately. Looking back, it really doesn't sound all that exciting, but the fact that this teacher I hardly knew gave me free rein on some of the stuff she had already assigned by the time I got there was pretty impressive. I also took an immediate role as her assistant in her classes to help familiarize myself with the material she was presenting and the students themselves.

I remember being somewhat overwhelmed by the level of trust that this teacher [Mrs Jones — a pseudonym] had in me. I hadn't really felt that she had evaluated me at all, and yet she felt comfortable letting me develop assignments for her classes on my own, and designing a few games for them to play (including a Jeopardy-like one for her top chemistry classes). Shortly after that I started teaching for her classes. Sometimes I taught OAC chemistry, sometimes I taught Grade 11 chemistry. It was up to me for the most part. Mrs Jones followed the textbooks for those two courses and so their texts became my primary resources. I also asked Mrs Jones for her help from time to time in designing lessons and she often offered her ideas as far as demos went from day to day.

At this stage I should provide a little background on my primary associate teacher (Mrs Jones) and her cohorts (or arch-rivals: it depends on your perspective really), Mr Brown and Mrs Hill. The teacher who agreed to take me on as a student-teacher was Mrs Jones, but that was because I approached her first (she was the chemistry department head). Mrs Jones was ＿＿＿ and a chemical engineer by degree (a female engineer thirty years ago was quite something). She had decided to go into teaching upon her arrival here in Canada (probably some thirty years ago). She had lived in ＿＿＿ for over twenty years previously. I think, at her core, she had some really traditional views about education, while she attempted to surround herself with contemporary views of learning. It was almost schizophrenic. One of the first things she did was to ask me why I wanted to be a teacher. I don't remember my answer exactly; I think it probably said something about my aptitudes in tutoring and my ability to create effective analogies. She responded with, 'If you don't love the kids, you won't get anywhere in this profession because, for a good teacher, this job is never about the money.' I remember that my heart soared when I heard that; little did I know about the flip-flops it would undergo later.

In any case, I soon began to see Mrs Jones not as the revolutionary educator she wanted me to see, but as the teacher she truly was. As I began to teach more and more lessons, Mrs Jones gave me more and more feedback. She encouraged me to take a stronger hand with discipline in the class. Especially with girls in the class! There was a group of three girls at the front of the Grade 11 chemistry class and she told me not to take any slack from them. When I observed her teaching, I saw her tactics, and I paid special attention to her actions towards these girls. Now, admittedly, the girls could be disruptive, and they demanded attention from whomever was teaching them. Whether or not that attention came in a positive or negative form didn't seem to make much difference. I began to notice that Mrs Jones was becoming more and more aggressive in her approach to tame these girls. She soon resorted to belittling them in front of the class. At first it was quite subtle. Soon her anger grew more overt and she became unable to control her outbursts herself. Mrs Jones would leave the class fuming. I remember one instance in particular when Mrs Jones yelled at Monica when she couldn't follow a math step that Mrs Jones had put on the board. Monica probably said something like, 'Miss, I don't understand any of that! I just don't get it!' In her frustration Mrs Jones told her to be quiet. She also ignored the question and the bell rang. Monica then told Mrs Jones that she couldn't follow her on the board, that she doesn't answer questions well — or something that Mrs Jones took personally directed at her teaching style. Monica could be obnoxious sometimes but I think it was because she didn't know better, not because she was malicious. Mrs Jones replied in a loud and condescending tone, 'It's not my job to teach you math. If you can't understand, you shouldn't be here!' Her voice got progressively louder. She had a furious temper. In any case, Monica became very visibly upset and started to yell back. I think that it was then that Mrs Jones called her 'dumb' or 'a stupid girl' and Monica, shaking and crying, ran out of the room. It all happened so quickly. That was the only time that I saw such a vicious confrontation, but it has left a lasting impression. This happened towards the middle of November. Within a few classes Monica was back to her normal self and didn't seem to harbor any ill feelings towards Mrs Jones. At the time I was amazed, but now I wonder if Monica didn't just decide that the whole incident had been her fault, that she had in some way deserved that belittlement. A truly scary thought. I never did have the courage to talk to Mrs Jones about that incident. I couldn't think of a good way of bringing it up without sounding as if I was judging her, and the last thing I wanted was her on my case. She had great respect for me in some areas (I showed her how to work miracles on computers) but in the field of classroom management I was always the rookie.

The really weird thing about the whole situation is that I still think that Mrs Jones really, REALLY loves all the kids she teaches. I think that somehow she thinks that she's just pushing the kids who are struggling to do better and that the only way to do that is to push them down a little. I think in the end she justifies it by thinking that she's doing these kids a great service or maybe even that it's her duty as a teacher to provide more negative than positive reinforcement to prepare them for the real world and all its expectations.

Mrs Jones also had two sons, and I noticed in her teaching that she tended to favor the boys in her classes. The boys were always 'smart' and 'intelligent' while the girls who answered well were 'lucky' sometimes, or at most 'good.' She was also about a hundred times more likely to overlook a mistake from a boy than she would the same mistake from a girl. That seemed pretty twisted to me since she herself was a woman with a degree in a male-dominated field (at least until lately). I attributed a large part of that to cultural differences.

As I taught more and more of the Grade 11 class, Mrs Jones began to get more and more afraid that I would turn them against her. I think she probably blamed me, at least in part, for the difficulties she was having with this class in the way of talking during class. Part of it could have been the fact that the class had to adjust to two totally different teaching styles, Mrs Jones's dictatorship, and my ever-changing teaching techniques. I can understand why they were a little unruly. The Grade 11s loved me. I was a pretty hard marker (Mrs Jones liked that) but I was fair. I told them what I expected and marked accordingly. It was tough sometimes, but one thing I wanted this class to learn was to live up to the expectations of an assignment. I also marked their labs rather hard. If I asked for titles and drawings and I gave them handouts with the names of all the chemicals, I took marks off if these things were missing or misspelt. I tried to be as comprehensive in my explanations before the lab was due as I could. During one lab in particular I was fairly strict on the observations that they wrote down and there was some discussion after the labs were handed back. I think that if I'd asked the class outright, they would've chosen me to teach them and Mrs Jones to mark them.

Mrs Jones considered herself to be fairly *au courant* when it came to science teaching issues. The Jeopardy-style game that I came up with was based on an idea that she got out of some teaching journal. I think that was the one thing that I truly admired about Mrs Jones, that she was still up on recent chemistry developments (from *Scientific American* and the like) and that she was pretty hip on finding neat activities. She wasn't afraid of trying new things with her classes as long as they didn't challenge her authority.

Those four months with Mrs Jones were some of the best and worst moments in my teaching career. The kids were always great. They were challenging, but bright, but most of all they were the first group of kids that I taught. The one thing that I really tried to focus on during those four months was classroom management skills. More than content, or pace, or interest level, I was worried that the classes would get out of control, or that they were headed (*albeit* slowly) towards anarchy. Mrs Jones helped to contribute to this fear, while teaching the Grade 9s in November helped to quash it. Mrs Jones contributed by worrying along with me. And most of the criticism I received from her concerned classroom management skills. 'So-and-so was talking — you should have told him to be quiet.' 'So-and-so was trying to monopolize your time, you should have told her to do her work.' Never did she tell me that any of that could have been because my lessons were too boring, or too teacher-centered, or inadequate. It was always something about discipline.

The Grade 9s were a task and a half. The range of kids in the class was indescribable. Mr Brown taught the Grade 9s before me. He was quite a character. He believed in the almighty 'show' of teaching. He didn't try to be a stand-up comic, or anything else as ridiculous as that, but he thought that you really needed to work on having presence at the front of the class. I think that in a lot of ways I've carried that attitude with me here. He also believed in discipline and was also getting up in years, but his discipline differed from Mrs Jones's. I don't remember him ever putting a kid down. He never had to. They were captivated by him. If they were too loud, he just told them to quiet down. They had respect for him.

I was another story altogether. They tested me. They didn't trust me. They didn't think I was a real teacher, exactly. And I had trouble being authoritative at the front of the class. I told kids to sit, over and over again. They knew that I would tell them five times before I really meant it, so they would wait and wait until they thought I'd get mad. They came around eventually. I tried slightly different approaches in my lesson presentation. I got a lot more organized before the lesson and tried to make my lessons more interactive, but in a way that would reinforce the structure of the lesson I wanted to create. I did a lot of handouts in those days. I also did quite a few demos. One thing that worked well was to give a handout, which required the kids to put a lot onto the piece of paper like drawings of apparatus (if it was a lab), or of molecules, or whatever. I also got a lot more serious with the material in the course. I gave a quiz that I had prepared in advance one day when they just wouldn't settle down. By the end of that month I had them eating out of the palm of my hand, and in retrospect I think that, as I became more of an authority figure and subsequently more comfortable in that role, it helped with the focus of my lessons and my presentation skills. I gave them a few pop quizzes in preparation for the Christmas exams. Some wouldn't count, they were strictly formative, but if I thought that they weren't listening to me or taking me seriously, I would collect them and mark them myself. I also got to make a great unit test.

By the end of December, as my four-month teaching placement neared its end, I had changed my theory vs practice impression once again. I'd had enough of practice. I'd had enough of teaching for a little while. I was feeling pretty burnt out. I also started to really believe that

Queen's would solve all my problems. I thought I'd go to a class and everyone would say what they did to get kids to be quiet and I'd listen, and I'd be the only one who'd had that problem, and there would be thirty solutions for me to choose from. I was basically ready for some theory. I also thought that learning about how kids learn would be a great asset to me as a teacher. For some reason I could envision all this happening in a large auditorium where some big expert tells me all I need to know about teaching in three hours or less. Ha, ha! This was my second big crisis. I didn't see much value in the experience I'd gained, other than the fact that it had helped me to identify the fact that I needed to work on classroom management.

Crisis 2 — I have experience, so now I'm ready to start learning about teaching.

My First Month at Queen's (January)

Queen's was totally different from what I expected. And what most of us expected, I think. In the beginning I still thought that some of those learning scenarios from above were really going to come through. I now thought that most of the ideas would come from us, but that some people would have their whole act together and all the right answers. I think that for a while in our sharing of experiences, that was almost what was happening. Everyone had some great way of doing something. I was beginning to think that teaching could be like some really complex recipe: if I could just follow it as closely as possible, and maybe throw in a few nuts instead of chocolate chips, I'd do great.

By the end of those five weeks I knew better. I felt like we really had started to carry the ball in a lot of our classes. Some of the best classes we had were ones in which I went away with more questions than I took in. That happened in a few classes, like the one where C____ did a role-play with S____ about a smart student whose grades start slipping. It got me thinking about myself and my teaching methods, not about the right way to deal with a student whose grades are slipping. I think that my teaching style and attitudes underwent a kind of revitalization because I had strayed a little off the path I started on in August, when I felt selfless. In those first four months, I was selfish. Now, at Queen's, I wanted to get back to a few ideals. I also began to get excited about putting some of the theory we talked about at Queen's into action during the imminent three-week placement. My definition of theory even underwent a change, from what a book tells you about teaching to what you can learn through discussion about teaching without actually setting foot in a classroom. By the end I was chomping at the bit to get out into a class again. I remember thinking that I had so many great demonstrations and approaches to try out, such as POE [Predict, Observe, Explain]. I had my moments of almost sheer terror when I thought about being a student-teacher again, but I was still pretty enthused overall. I thought that I'd be much better at classroom management issues too.

Crisis 3 — Why am I still 'carrying the ball' so much, as I learn to teach?

Three More Weeks of Teaching (February)

I didn't really know what to expect going into these three weeks. I was glad that I hadn't gone back to my old high school in those first four months, because I had already faced the task of integrating myself into a new school once. Yet I was still concerned about what it would be like to be a substitute teacher for three weeks.

This shorter teaching assignment was a really great learning experience for me, in a way that I didn't think it would be. I started to really think about the nature of science and scientific theories. We talked about it at Queen's, but I didn't really see then how it was important. Teaching evolution really showed me how little I knew about the development of science.

Ted, my associate, also had a completely different perspective on classroom management issues than Mrs Jones did. One of the first things that he said to the two of us (we were assigned in pairs, as 'critical friends') was that he wouldn't mind if we just ignored the whole classroom management thing. He also had a really laid-back attitude when it came to teaching and teaching styles. As well, he was also pretty open-minded when it came to pedagogy.

It ended up that I didn't have to do any classroom management. Part of that was due to the teachers who taught the students before and after I was there, but I think part of it was me, too. As practicum progressed, I also began to consider my T1 experience in a different light. For me, it became a great example of a lot of the things I never want to do. Previously I think that I viewed it more as a kind of feet-wetting experience so that I would know what was going on when I got to Queen's. Now I had the opportunity to develop a teaching style on my own, and the more experience I get teaching, the better able I am to shape and refine that style. Thanks to Mrs Jones and Mr Brown I have a pretty good idea of what I definitely don't want to be like when I start teaching. Looking back on some of the teaching I did I also have an idea of what I don't want to start teaching like again. I never really thought of it that way before.

These three weeks also gave me the chance to change the way I presented material to the classes. I tried the approach Ted used with the oldest students, an approach that involves lecturing without notes that are word for word, challenging the students to really think and gauging their progress verbally, and attempting to give the students a glimpse of the big picture daily. I really tried to give them insight into what they needed to take away from my lessons about each unit.

Now I don't expect to get answers from anyone any more — especially not a textbook. I think all the really profound answers come from within, sometimes with the guidance of others, sometimes not. I also think that I'm going to need a lot more experience teaching before I can be really happy with my teaching style. It's going to take some work.

Crisis 4 — Experience Really is the Best Kind of Learning.

More Time at Queen's (March to April)

Over the last few weeks I haven't experienced any more crises, and this is a crisis in itself, really. Lately everything just seems to be getting wrapped up and our classes are winding down. I can't believe my time here at Queen's is almost done!

I'm not naive enough now to think that I'm done learning about teaching. I'm finally totally convinced it's going to be a lifelong process. I just hope I can keep my enthusiasm level up! I've never kept a journal for any significant length of time, although the idea has always appealed to the romantic in me. The one I kept over the four months just wasn't personal enough for me to feel it was worthwhile. I'm looking forward to starting one up. And I'm going to start it soon. Reading over my journal kept for a course here at Queen's reminds me of how significant an experience journal writing can be, and there's so much about Queen's that I don't want to forget. Two great motivating factors.

Those three weeks two months ago are starting to seem more and more distant, never mind the four months last fall or the next four months still eight months away. I'm really glad that I had the opportunity to write all this down in a story-type format as a reminder of some of the things I've learned along the way. Just a little bit of Queen's I can go back to every once in a while until I graduate.

Crisis 5 — There's No Crisis!

Finally, I see now that I've come full circle in my quest for learning how to teach. From the perspective I have now, after many significant teaching experiences and insights, I find myself returning to the simple and intuitive.

Chapter 8

Finding My Voice as an English Teacher

Dawn Bellamy

Overview

Dawn Bellamy is a teacher of English in Wiltshire in England. Through Jack Whitehead, who introduced her to action research during her PGCE (Post-Graduate Certificate in Education) course at the University of Bath, Dawn has had opportunities to meet each of the co-editors of this collection at conferences on teacher education and educational research since 1994. We are very pleased to include here this account of her perspectives on professional voice as she looks back over her year-long initial training course and her first two years as a 'newly qualified teacher.'

Learning to Teach

This story begins almost fifteen years ago, when I decided at age 11 that I wanted to be an English teacher. At that point, everything made sense. I loved English and I loved school, so what better career choice could possibly lie ahead for me? Now, at age 25, I have been in the classroom full-time for two years and am anticipating my third year in the same school, an 11–18 mixed comprehensive school in Wiltshire, England. I often wonder if I would have made my early decision had I known exactly what faced me on my journey towards becoming a teacher. If only things could have remained as simple as they appeared to be when I was 11! The reality, however, as I have come to understand it, is that unexpected surprises can catch me unawares at any point in time, no matter how well prepared I am. Two years in the classroom have certainly taught me that. The story I tell here is intended to share insights into my own personal experience of finding a voice while learning to teach.

As it stands at the moment, my story seems naturally to fall into three main sections. It is important for me to say at this point that I do not consider that I have *learned* to teach. I still perceive myself as *learning* to teach, using my daily experiences to fuel the process of becoming rather than being. For me, one aspect of finding a professional voice involves coming to a better understanding of myself: it is an issue of *self-recognition*. The realization that learning to teach is an ongoing process occurred during my pre-service year at Bath University in 1993–94, and it is there that I begin my story.

Bath University Post-Graduate Certificate in Education Course (PGCE): 1993–94

When I heard that I had been admitted to the course at Bath, I was overwhelmed. I had been accepted at my first choice of university and I knew that I would have thirty-six weeks to learn as much as I could about teaching. The brevity of the course concerned me. I wasn't quite sure that anyone could learn to teach in such a short time, but I had heard that the course was one of the best and was therefore quite confident that I would be told all I needed to know. I had enjoyed my undergraduate studies at Leicester University and felt that it was time to move on, to try somewhere new and to get on with the process of entering my chosen career.

It was hard to be a 'new girl' again. Leaving familiar, safe surroundings in which I had been successful gave me a few qualms, and my nerves were exacerbated by my realization that I was one of the youngest people on the English course at Bath. I was also one of the few who was not entering teaching having worked in industry or overseas. While I did not think that this would necessarily be a problem, it did little to help me to silence the inner voice that kept asking, 'Am I doing the right thing?' It was a question that never entirely disappeared during my time at Bath and it is one that I still find myself asking at intervals. As someone who views herself as a thoughtful and reflective practitioner, I do not see this question as problematic: As long as I can keep working things through until I can answer 'Yes,' then I am not troubled by this manifestation of my voice. What happens when the answer is constantly 'No'? I hope that I will have the integrity to move on, as there are many more people involved in this enterprise than the 'I' to which I am drawn to listen.

Although I am sure that the people who know me now would find this hard to believe, when I am unsure of myself I find it difficult to challenge those people I perceive to be in positions of authority. Know-ing this has, I hope, an impact on my practice, as I try to encourage pupils to question my actions and decisions if they feel that issues need clarification. It is my intention to make my pupils feel comfortable enough with my classroom environment (not necessarily in any aes-thetic sense, although this inevitably has some impact on the situation) that they can overcome any fears of challenging my position of author-ity. Obviously, I am keen to establish parameters concerning appropri-ate forms of challenge, yet as a result of my own fears (I hate going to see a doctor as I am constantly aware of his 'authority' over me in terms of his specialist knowledge), I aim to dissolve any such feelings in my classroom.

At the beginning of my PGCE course at Bath, I was eager to do things properly. I suppose that I aimed to please, as I perceived that as the road to success. During the course of the year I came to realize that to be a successful teacher I would have to be a strong individual. There would be things that I might have to fight for in the future. With all the impositions from the outside, I was afraid that I would soon be teach-ing a particular lesson on a particular day in a way set down by some-body outside my classroom. Such a potential future made me afraid. I had to learn to stand up for myself. Although at the time I was infuri-ated by the events taking place, the course took shape in such a way that did push me to make a stand — to find my voice.

The details of my frustrations and struggles with the PGCE course are set out in a piece of work I completed during that year, 'The Kaleidoscope Rainbow: How can I help Thomas to increase his flex-ibility as a learner so that he shows the same assuredness in his writing as in his speaking? An Action Enquiry' (Bellamy, 1994). I do not want to revisit the finer details here. Suffice it to say that my reflections on the course changed in tone. Here is one of my early journal entries:

> It is important to understand the provisions made for Learning Sup-port within the establishment in which you are working so that appro-priate action can be taken when necessary. It is reassuring to learn that so much support is available for teachers whose classes contain pupils with learning difficulties. (October 1993)

Mid-way through the course, during a term of teaching practice, I wrote this:

> I was slightly sceptical to begin with about the relevance of this task to my professional development . . . I approached it with a lack of commitment. (February 1994)

As we moved beyond the halfway point of the course I recorded these thoughts:

> It makes me so furious to think that this is intended to satisfy us . . . the deadlines have been in place for ages and, much as I dislike the pressure and resent the way in which I am being forced to hand in work with which I am dissatisfied, I have worked to these deadlines and now feel that I am being punished for the effort! . . . I am learning that nothing is ever straightforward. (March 1994)

Looking back at these entries exemplifies for me the way in which I began to find my voice as I was learning to teach. The early entry contains nothing of myself; it is a detached piece of writing in which I deal merely with the topic being studied in that week's tutorial. The February statement shows that I am beginning to articulate my own feelings about the work we were being asked to do. There is an honesty about my reflections at this stage which suggests that I was becoming more confident of my own voice and my right to be heard. The final entry was written at a point in time when I could no longer contain myself. I had no doubts about my right to be heard at this moment and I wanted to *make* people listen to me. That particular piece of journal writing ended with a speculative comment:

> Perhaps . . . I am learning a lot about my own strength of commitment to this course and also about my own educational values. As long as I remain open to such learning about my own development, I believe that I will be more able to communicate the values in which I believe within the classroom. (March 1994)

I cared too much about becoming a teacher to allow the frustrations of an over-burdened assessment program within the course to defeat me. I had found my voice and was aware that I could benefit from listening to it. This may prove how much trust I was willing to place in my own beliefs. Of course, the levels of trust in my own voice have fluctuated regularly since that time, but what exists at the root of all my highs and lows is *a fundamental belief that what I am doing is right.* I am not advocating the denial of doubt, for I believe that doubt prompts many of the questions I am led to ask myself about my practice as an educator. Jack Whitehead, one of my PGCE tutors at Bath, explains his notion of a living educational theory by stating:

> I am arguing for a reconstruction of educational theory into a living form of question and answer. (1993, p. 68)

By questioning elements of my practice, I am encouraged to move forward by finding answers to those questions in subsequent practice. I aim to hear my own voice and use it in order to generate improvements within my teaching. As Jean McNiff suggests:

> Teaching and learning are two sides of the same coin; they are two perspectives of the same process. (1993, p. 59)

In my year at Bath University I actually began to understand this statement. I was learning to teach, and teaching at the same time. I was learning about myself as a learner and myself as a teacher, and I was beginning to shape my future through such a perspective. I had found my voice during the course, being driven to shouting about my own needs by a program that seemed to deny the needs of the individuals participating, while expecting its pre-service teachers to recognize the needs of each pupil within their classrooms. At the end of the course I was extremely disillusioned: Was I really prepared to go into the classroom full time? At the time I would probably have answered 'No,' although I knew that it was still what I wanted to do. What I realize now is that going through that process of finding my voice helped me immensely in the sense that it confirmed my beliefs in an educational system that listened to those people involved and tried to work with them rather than against them. Those are the ideals that I carried forward with me into my first year as a qualified teacher.

Wootton Bassett School: 1994–95

I was in a relatively unusual position when I started my first year of teaching at Wootton Bassett School because I had done the majority of my teaching practice there as part of my PGCE course. I had the advantages of knowing the geography of the school, of knowing some of the staff and pupils, and of understanding some of the systems in place in the English Faculty. Regardless of everything that was 'known,' I was still extremely nervous when I arrived at the school on my first day. No longer had I the safety net of a university course to catch me if I fell, and I was inevitably unsure of my ability to do it 'for real.' Once again I was a 'new girl' and I was aware that I would have to re-start, *albeit* from a different position, the process of finding a voice. In my reflections on my new role, even from an early stage, my voice is evident:

> The difficulties with timetabling are driving me mad! What good is it to be told just to relax and wait to see which class turns up? I can't

> work like that, not yet anyway. It's as if I'm not an NQT [Newly
> Qualified Teacher], and that is really frustrating. (6 September 1994)

However, even as I write this chapter I am uncertain about including such journal entries. I am still wary of confronting authority and I feel that making public such personal writing may challenge people who could react unfavourably towards me and make my working life uncomfortable. As a young person in a profession, I am constantly confronted by this issue. It frustrates me immensely, and I gain great satisfaction from the moments when I essentially throw caution to the wind and speak my mind. However, finding the courage to speak out against those in authority has not come easily to me, despite my firm belief in my right to question decisions that involve me. Even at such an early stage in my career I was experiencing what I then termed the 'dilemma of an NQT under pressure' (6 September 1994) and it is this dilemma that has not been, and may never be, fully resolved.

Even though, at university, I had reached a point at which I felt I *had* to make my voice public, I was, and still am at times, unable to do this in school. What had changed? Perhaps I felt isolated and vulnerable at school in a way I had not at Bath. I knew that I had a point at Bath and felt able to argue it, even with the Director of Studies at one stage! The vulnerability of my position is still not entirely clear to me: Of what am I afraid? There had been a certain fearlessness about my actions at university that I could not rediscover as I stepped into the classroom for the first time as a qualified teacher. I wonder how many experienced teachers recall such a feeling. Is it common? If so, surely those people who are responsible for the mentoring of Newly Qualified Teachers should seek ways of addressing this at an early point in a teacher's career, because the pressure can and does build up.

September 1994 found me feeling uncertain in a way that I did not recognize. When I started at Bath in the previous September, I was a postgraduate; I had been at university for three years already and had been a learner in an educational setting since the age of 4. Suddenly, in beginning to teach, I seemed to be in a totally new situation. Tom Russell (1993) writes about his research with Hugh Munby:

> We believe that new teachers should be shown how to recognize and develop the authority of personal experience . . . It requires a willingness and an ability to listen to one's own experiences. (p. 4)

While I was willing to listen to my own experiences, I was unable to place any trust in the authority of my own experience because I was no longer receiving any feedback. One of the strengths of the Bath course for me was that I was given regular feedback about my teaching and plenty of opportunities to discuss my practice with my mentor as I learned to teach. On my own in a classroom, it seemed as if my learning had stopped. I had not learned to interpret my own learning. The opportunities for structured reflection had more or less disappeared, and although I was keeping a fairly regular journal — something that would become less and less frequent as the year progressed — no one was helping me to 'develop the authority of personal experience' by engaging in regular dialogue about my first year of teaching. Yes, there were snatched conversations and brief enquiries about how the classes were going, but time was scarce and talking about teachers' experiences in classrooms seemed to be very low on the professional agenda.

Once again, I had a feeling I had experienced during my PGCE. There seemed to be a lack of correlation between what was being offered to teachers and what was being offered to learners. The experience I was having appeared to deny that I was in fact still very much a learner, *albeit* an adult learner. I had always been told about the importance of praise when assessing pupils' work. I truly believed that in order to encourage pupils to make further progress I should focus on what they had done well and then set them some targets for the future, giving them some confidence in their own abilities while providing a framework for continued progress. Why was no one praising my initial efforts? Surely there had to be a fault somewhere in a system that does allow its NQTs to be educated via a partnership between a university and schools, in a system that instead withdraws any formalized support. Would I sink or would I swim?

In many ways I see now that I swam. I can look back at journal entries for my first half term as a qualified teacher and see that I was beginning to find my voice in the classroom:

> It's amazing how I can diversify more easily these days; how I can slip into another activity more smoothly . . . I think it's all to do with confidence . . . (14 September 1994)

> One of the main changes I've noticed in the shift from Novice Teacher to Newly Qualified Teacher is that there's so much more flexibility. I was a confident Novice Teacher (I think) but I tended to do things I thought my mentors would like. What's the point? It's then quite a shock to get into your first job and realise that the teaching-practice me was nothing much like the qualified me. (30 September 1994)

As I reflected on my classroom experiences I was able to recognize the emergence of a new, more confident voice, and much of this came from the piece of paper that told me I was a qualified teacher of English. However, I believe that despite the lack of time for structured reflection I was beginning to become aware of the authority of my own experience. Some of this was resulting from my work with the children and the relationships that were developing within the classroom. I noted a significant moment in my journal:

> She seemed to be having trouble understanding exactly what was needed so we approached it from several angles until she began to make the connections for herself. It was her comment as she went to sit down that made the difference though: 'If I don't quite get it I can always come and ask you again.' . . . She felt secure enough to make that suggestion. (15 October 1994)

It was not only my interactions with pupils that were helping me to believe in myself. I had established regular e-mail contact with Derek Featherstone and Tom Russell in Ontario in Canada, and this was helping me to reflect in a more communal sense with people outside my immediate environment yet within education. Our correspondence became quite a lifeline for me during my first year of teaching, as I was able to express myself without the inhibitions imposed by institutional etiquette and to receive responses which reassured, reinforced, challenged and enabled me to move my thinking forward in ways I was not encountering at school. More than anything else, writing to Tom and Derek (along with Mary Lynn Hamilton and Stefinee Pinnegar in Kansas and Utah in the USA) helped me to overcome the sense of isolation I had been feeling since qualifying as a teacher and heading out into the 'big wide world'. I think I needed to feel part of something much bigger, something that would have an impact outside of my classroom, something that would give my work some meaning. I know now from my present situation, just entering my third year of teaching, that some of my favourite moments since entering the profession have been spent in the company of Tom, Derek, Stefinee and Mary Lynn (amongst others) at the American Educational Research Association meeting in New York (April 1996), and at the first international conference on Self-Study of Teacher Education Practices held at Herstmonceux Castle, England (August 1996). For me, these people constitute a community of educators who reflect on and study their own practices in ways that have given me a framework for looking at my own experiences. Their support and feedback during my first year of teaching provided the reflective fix that I needed, helping me to learn to listen to the authority of my own experience and therefore enabling the emergence of the voice that would begin to speak in different ways during my second year in the classroom.

Wootton Bassett School: 1995–96

Much of what I have written about so far seems to relate to my own questions about professional identity as I struggled to come to terms with myself as a teacher. I had had twenty-three years to come to understand myself as a learner before I entered into the enterprise of teaching, and that shift created a number of instabilities that I must resolve in due course and that I continue to engage. Retrospectively, I can see that at the outset I was expecting to become someone new, someone different. It was as if I would put on my new 'teacher's hat' and would suddenly change into someone I had never been before. I can look back now and judge myself as naive although I am sure I am not the only new entrant into a profession who has felt that things would look vastly different beneath the mantle of qualifications. However, as I try now to think about ways in which I found my voice during my second year of teaching I am drawn to a story in which elements of my old self began to reassert itself — my self as a learner. Before this episode took place I had begun to believe that my teacher-self was in fact a metamorphosis of myself as a learner. Teaching is, for me, such a personal profession — a job which relies so much upon who I am and what I believe — that I could not fail to hear the voice I had heard so many times before. I was just listening from within a new context, hearing during a range of new experiences, and speaking from a different position.

In my second year of teaching I was given an 'A' level English Literature class for the first time. I looked forward to the challenge of teaching 16-year-olds — students who had chosen to be in my classroom rather than having to be there as part of their National Curriculum studies. I knew that I would have opportunities to teach texts I had enjoyed studying at an advanced level, and that lessons would be slightly different from those with larger classes lower down the school because they would be conducted in something more akin to the tutorial style I had enjoyed at university. While I was nervous and felt the weight of the responsibility of helping students to achieve grades that would enable them to proceed to university, I was relishing the thought of discussing literature on a level different from that explored with classes of younger students.

One day one of my 'A' level students came to me asking for help with a text she had been asked to study for a summer school she would be attending. I happened not to be teaching at the time and was able to spend some time there and then discussing the poem with her. It was wonderful! For almost an hour we talked about literature. We focused closely on the text and moved beyond it to discuss ways of reading, ways of looking at the world. We voiced our ambitions and our hopes for the future, and we connected on a level I have only rarely experienced since entering the classroom.

I believe that what happened in those brief moments spent looking at T.S. Eliot's *The Waste Land* helped me to find, perhaps to rediscover, my voice in one of the most exciting ways open to a teacher. In talking with my student I was able to blend elements of my past self with my present self, and to experience something that would inevitably affect my future self. I became a literature student once again, putting forward tentative ideas, responding to another's thoughts about a text, and immersing myself in the ambiguities of a piece of writing that could mean one thing to me and something completely different to the person I was helping. I use the word 'helping' deliberately, as it was her request for help that reinforced my position as teacher in that particular relationship. While on one level we could share something as fellow lovers of literature, there was another level on which I would hear my voice from another perspective. It was at this point that I became aware of the ways in which the many elements of my self were merging. While I could offer my student insights I had learned or discovered during my years as an undergraduate (returning to my past), I could only do so in such a way because I was involved in a teacher–student relationship with her (my present self). What I was doing was trying to help her to move forward in terms of increasing her understanding of a poem. However, the ways in which I was able to do this involved a complex combination of selves and voices.

That moment was extremely important to me. It marks a point at which I realized that I had a voice people wanted to hear. The student had come to ask for *my* help. I had performed a professional function in what seemed to me an intensely personal way; asking and answering questions, making tentative suggestions, and admitting to utter confusion about a piece of literature. What has happened to me at the beginning of my third year of teaching in terms of my timetable and the subjects I have been asked to teach has proved to me just how important being a teacher of English is to who I am. In response to one of my e-mail messages, Tom Russell replied:

I'm beginning to think that you love English teaching so much, and your desire to teach is so firmly associated with your love of English, that the prospect of being asked to 'be teacher' in a subject you have not studied just makes no sense at all to you . . . It leaves you knowing, deep down, that you WILL be a 'living contradiction' no matter what you do, because the subject has no meaning or reality for you. You are just being asked to 'go through the motions of being a teacher'. (Tom Russell, personal communication, 17 September 1996)

Having looked back at the ways in which I have found my voice while learning to teach, I am drawn to conclusions that link who I was before I started teaching to who I am at this point in time. As a result of this, I can only reinforce what Tom suggested in his response to my complaint at having been asked to teach outside of my subject area. My voice comes from deep within me. It reflects who I am because who I am has so much bearing upon the way I choose to act in the classroom.

I do not believe that the quest for my professional voice has ended or is indeed in any way finite. I still struggle to speak out in certain situations and will endeavour to approach these in ways that will allow my voice to emerge so that it does not compromise my identity. I made a resolution at the First International Conference on Self-Study of Teacher Education Practices held at Herstmonceux Castle in August 1996, and that resolution was to speak out professionally. This interim account of my development as a teacher represents the first step towards keeping that resolution. I hope that I have spoken to you as you join me in learning to teach.

References

BELLAMY, D. (1994) 'The Kaleidoscope Rainbow: How can I help Thomas to increase his flexibility as a learner so that he shows the same assuredness in his writing as in his speaking — An Action Enquiry.' Unpublished manuscript, University of Bath, UK.

McNIFF, J. (1993) *Teaching as Learning: An Action Research Approach*, London, Routledge.

RUSSELL, T. (1993, June) 'Recognizing the authority of experience: Returning to the physics classroom to re-think how one learns to teach physics.' Paper presented to the meeting of the Canadian Society for the Study of Education, Ottawa.

WHITEHEAD, J. (1993) *The Growth of Educational Knowledge: Creating Your Own Educational Theories*, Bournemouth, UK, Hyde Publications.

Chapter 9

Students as Critical Friends: Helping Students Find Voices

Derek Featherstone and Grade 10 Science Students

Introduction

During two years of teacher education and my first year of teaching, I have written personal accounts of my teaching and learning experiences with a group of critical friends. Several of these papers have explored the relationships of some of the partnerships in education that can exist. For example, Peter Chin, Tom Russell and I have written papers that describe and outline the ways we study our teaching together through interactive electronic-mail conversations (see Chapter 10). In these conversations, we look at what we are able to learn from each other and how our interactions help us to improve our teaching in our respective classrooms. We are able to gain new insights from each other in terms of the universality of the issues that we face. We also find that a critical view from outside our own environment helps us to see how our teaching practices relate to our educational objectives. We are particularly interested in views that highlight ways in which our teaching practices may be counter-productive to our goals.

As the title of this chapter indicates, I have put a new spin on the idea of 'critical friends' who help me understand my teaching. In this chapter I explore the possibility of my students being my critical friends. Although I had no clue as to where I should start, I did know that I wanted to include the student voice in my work as part of my personal reflective process. At several recent conferences, I had been literally 'attacked' (verbally!) for not including my students' perspective in accounts of my teaching, and those attacks made me try to avoid this aspect of reflective writing. I felt that if I gave in to that pressure, then my critics would have achieved their goal. Yet it was not until I was approached by Garry Hoban (Charles Sturt University, New South Wales) and Tom Russell (Queen's University) to work on a project to encourage students to document their learning processes that I considered the possibility.

Rather than 'force-feeding' the idea to me, they presented 'students as critical friends' in an exciting and logical way that captured my interest, reminding me yet again that how something is presented can make all the difference. As I think about why I am now willingly involved in this type of inquiry, I wonder how the material that I am presenting as I teach appears to my students. If I was put off by the fact that I perceived suggestions as being imposed on me, what implications does that personal reaction have for how my students react to what I present in my classes? I see that, for my students to willingly engage in a course, I cannot present things as though I am 'forcing them to learn'.

This chapter is based on a five-day teaching episode with one of my classes at Ashbury College, Ottawa, in this, my second year of teaching. I try to present my own reflections and my students' reflections, the reflections of a colleague, as well as the process of reflection itself as it relates to the idea of collaborating with *students as critical friends*. I also try to weave a dialogue that depicts how what was happening from my perspective relates to the perspectives of my students. Finally, I try to articulate specific points I have learned from this inquiry, and how they relate to being a critically reflective teacher.

The Idea and the Opportunity

On 6 October 1996 I spoke with my good friend and colleague, Tom Russell, about this project. I knew that I wanted to have my students help me to reflect on what I was doing in the classroom, but I was unsure of the parameters of the study, what data I should be collecting as evidence, and generally how I should get started. Tom suggested that the dialogue between my students and I could be centred around a classroom event that I saw as educationally significant. I could then get them to write about it, and I would have a starting point for discussion. The opportunity suddenly became clear to me in class on 11 October.

I felt that we, as a class, had reached a very significant point in the year. The assignment was set up so that the students could be creative. I had outlined the basic content of the process of natural succession. In simple terms, natural succession is the natural progression and change in the dominant vegetation of a geographic area. For example, an abandoned farmer's field will quickly sprout several different species of grasses. Following that, there is a progression from grasses to small weeds, to woody perennial plants, to small shrubs, and finally to small trees, until the area becomes a forest consisting of different species of larger trees and undergrowth. With this much 'on the table,' it was up to the students to take over and represent this process in a creative way that showed me that they understood the process of natural succession.

When I made the assignment, I did not indicate that a presentation was required. There was only one student who seemed keen to present work to the class on the day it was due, and I had expected this level of response. I did not expect many to volunteer because it was still relatively early in the year, and there is significant risk in getting up in front of one's peers to make a creative presentation. While the first student was setting up, others began to rise to the occasion and offered to present their projects. By the time we were done, most of the class had presented. In some cases, I asked permission to present the work on behalf of students who did not seem willing to present on their own. Other students offered to sing back-up for a song that one of their classmates had written. We saw a skit, and one student did a mobile. There were two three-dimensional models, at least two comic books, and even a cook book. All the projects presented natural succession very creatively.

I was astounded with both the product and the educational process that the students had just been through. I have never seen such instantaneous camaraderie from a class. After the presentations, I recalled the conversation with Tom earlier in the week and made a snap decision to use this teaching episode as a starting point for engaging with my students as critical friends. I asked them to write about this event. They didn't feel they knew what to write, so I suggested that they write about whatever they wanted to — how they felt when I first assigned the project, how they felt while they were working on their project, how they felt now, what they had learned. I saw the event as something educationally significant for them and for me. As they wrote, I completed the following journal entry:

> I have just asked all of my students to write about what just took place in class, so I think it is appropriate that I write too. We had set the task to learn about natural succession and represent the content in a creative way. I was astounded by the projects that were turned in due to the incredible variety and scope of the material — ranging from 3D models, to a mobile, a comic book or two, a cook book, songs, paintings, poetry, and an incredible analogy. I have not experienced anything like this before.
>
> I wonder now what would happen if I did this again. Would more people do different creative things? Will they feed off each others' creativity? I presented on behalf of a few people who didn't want to present themselves — of course, with their permission. Their work was received quite well by the rest of the class. I wonder if they would present next time?

I have learned a lot from this — first and foremost is that I believe that I am setting an appropriate cooperative tone in the class. Setting Mr F's BIG 4 [classroom rules] at the start of the year sure helps. We've made it obvious that we can't make fun of each other, *and* that we should celebrate our successes together. I wonder how many students find that to be more significant than the learning about succession itself?

The basic content was there — of course some details were missing, but I'll sacrifice some details for the major concept of succession getting across. Their responses that I've asked them to write should certainly make for some interesting learning for me. (11 October 1996)

After we had all taken the time to write about the experience, I asked the students if they would mind sharing their responses. They seemed very eager to do so. Many of them read aloud what they had written, with some paraphrasing. Hearing their words was instantly gratifying, although the full impact of what they had written did not hit me until I actually typed their words into a file myself. (Note that some members of this group do not speak English as a first language.) Here is what they wrote:

The things that comes to my mind about the project that we did in the class was [that it was] very interesting to me because I had learned about how the forest starts and how it can end. Just like the way that the story that was told started and ended. The first thing that got me really interested was [Student 5s] story — it teaches how a poor man (like bare rocks) became rich (like a tree in a forest). His story was very interesting and amazing too. (Student 1)

We studied about natural succession using the text book so that we can know about it very well. But to be frank, that way is not interesting — a little boring. Today's exercise was very interesting and funny — sing a song about natural succession, comics, Mr Natural Succession, poems, etc. . . . So the knowledge is not just knowledge. We can apply it anywhere. It was very good, and everybody was perfect. (Student 2)

I like it. Everyone made good project. We had a good time, and I could understand about succession. They sang a song, draw picture and made it to explain to us. I was so interesting and made it fun. It helped me to study succession. Our classmates did hard. AND I also tried hard. But I don't know my project is good or not. Anyway . . . Great. (Student 3)

I think this is very nice to us. We can understand well. This was funny and nice to me. Other guys did really nice and very well. Mine is very simple stuff and bad drawing but I understand what is succession. (Student 4)

I'm feel very proud to myself and happy with my classmates because they worked very hard and made the teacher very happy. He said the word that I don't know how to spell but I know it means it was very good. It make my day was specially. I learned a lot of things that helped me to prove myself and give me more information about succession, that is, how forest is come and ended. And the project we did in the class showed me that the time can change your life or environment. I'm happy to be in this science class. That was very interesting and very funny and nice. Thank you so much. *Deemak*!!! ['Deemak' is the English spelling for a Thai word. Earlier I had asked [Student 5] how I would tell him that he had done a good job on something. He has taught me how to say a few important phrases in Thai, and to write 'deemak' in Thai so that I can write it on his papers. I believe he is telling me here that he is really pleased with my teaching of this subject.] (Student 5)

I learned about succession, but more than that I learned that science can be fun. While we could have been asked to learn about succession by answering questions from a textbook, Mr Featherstone gave us something interesting to do making us more inclined to learn. Last year [our teacher] didn't do anything like this and the class was really boring. This year's science class is funner, not only because of this cool project, but because every class is more interesting. And I've probably learned more this way. The presentations were really hilarious and creative. Mr Featherstone, you are a very cool teacher!!! (Student 6)

I learned many things from doing this activity. These included how thoroughly we would have to understand something to be able to do an activity like this, how to be creative, to what extent we would have to work to have a good result on something, and how to perform in front of a crowd. In the beginning of this activity, I thought that it would be a fun activity. However, as the days went on I thought deeply of how my presentation would be (if we had to do one). I seriously thought that my presentation of the song was going to be terrible and embarrassing. After the activity, while I am writing this, I realize how important something like this is. *I thank you very much for introducing us to such an activity.* This really improved my experience of how to do something in front of a crowd because I learned that, even if I think what I am going to do is bad, there is no extent to how bad something can be, and therefore, it should not hurt to go and do something in front of the class. (Student 7)

I thought it was a really cool and innovative idea to let us be creative and think about what we were learning in Science. The class also came up with cool and innovative ideas for presenting their work. Personally I really love presenting stuff in front of people — that's why I want to be a lawyer!! But I seriously think that it was really great the way that some people just got up there and even if they were embarrassed, managed to show the class what great work they did. I think it would be awesome if we did some more stuff like this for other topics (but not straight away!) because it really makes you understand the concepts. Whoever said that people are visual was totally right. Anyway, it was a really interesting and fun way to learn. (Student 8)

What I learned about succession: Before I did this project on succession, I had no idea what it was. I wanted to make a model of what happened in the steps to illustrate the different changes that happen over time. I enjoyed making the model because I like to create things with my mind and my hands. Because I did primary succession I was sort of aware of the other kinds (i.e., secondary succession) but after listening and seeing the results of other people's ideas it has made things much more clear. I liked every one of the presentations and I am not just saying that. (Student 9)

Succession project: fun. If we did it again it would be even better because no one would be embarrassed. It was easy but I still learned a lot. It made the classroom atmosphere more relaxed. It presented the information in so many different ways that no matter which way someone learns best, they would have learned it well. (Student 10)

What I learned! When I first was told about the idea I did not know what to do. I found that there were so many possible ideas I could have come up with. I then thought to myself that by taking an idea like a comic book I could make it seem like a real comic book by making the pictures seem professional and writing a fairly decent dialogue. Probably the most important thing that I learned is that I now know for certain that it is possible to learn or to be educated while having a lot of fun and thoroughly enjoying it. Also when I first learned about the project I was thinking of making a video, but with the freedom we had with this project I was able to bridge both a written product as well as an illustrated one. (Student 11)

From these projects I learned many things about succession. The projects were amazing, especially [Student 8's]. People put a lot of time and effort into these projects and their work paid off. The people who actually had the guts to go up and present their projects should be congratulated. This was my idea of a class! We should do more projects like this! These exercise was much more fun than just sitting around in class taking down notes off of the blackboard. In my opinion, the idea of succession sunk in better this way than any other. I also learned that [Student 7] has no career as a singer (sorry Student 7!!). Mr Featherstone is a really cool teacher in that his projects are fun to do and he likes professional wrestling (and the television show *Beasties*!!). (Student 12)

[Student 7] can't sing. [Student 8] is amazing. I have to be more creative to compare! I like it from the start. Life is good. Succession is good. I learned a lot of related terms. [Student 7] really can't sing! I could have done better [on my project]. The presentations gave me a better understanding. I wish I could be outside in the grass. During this class it was harder to be preoccupied and aloof — I paid complete attention! It's hot in here when everyone is moving around and laughing at [Student 7's] singing. Presentations were fun to watch. More classes should have this much student intervention. (Student 13)

I learned that it was very fun be able to create your own things without limitations. At the start, I wasn't sure what I should have done but an idea did end up coming to me. I thought that this exercise was very fun and brought out our creative side. I hope that we will do more of them in the future. (Student 14)

At the start of this project I was a bit 'iffy' about what I was going to do. But I found something to do and had fun doing it. I guess I also learned about primary succession along the way too. I also learned that school can be fun. I don't like standing up in front of a class because I'm very shy but it was really funny to watch other people and their wide range of ideas and it was a fun project to work on. (Student 15)

At the beginning, I thought that this was kind of a stupid project because I thought that no one in the class would really care about it and get it done the period before it was due. I also thought that I wouldn't come up with good ideas and if I did, people would make fun of it. The songs, the cookbook, [Student 5's] story and everything else really surprised me that people would do that kind of stuff and take their time to do it too. I liked how this assignment wasn't a completely serious assignment — we could have fun with it. I was just really amazed [at the amount] of fun you can make a serious subject be and that what people did today really showed that. I liked how everyone accepted other's ideas and didn't make fun of them. It encourages me to do something like that next time and not being afraid of doing what I want. (Student 16)

At this point, I was absolutely thrilled with what I had seen in the classroom. Over the next few days, I took the time to document my reflections in my journal:

> . . . based on recent classroom experiences . . .
> One thing that I would like to do in my own teaching is to develop some sort of discussion summary sheet. This was sparked by one of my students making a comment about the creative succession assignment, and several stages of reframing the experience afterwards.
>
> After all of the students and I had written about the experience of the project, we took about five minutes to share what each other had written. It was, of course, optional. After several comments, one student said that although she didn't write this down she thought that it was important that I 'don't think that learning only takes place if we are taking lots of notes.' This made me think more about the nature of the classroom atmosphere that I have tried to foster. I can't help but think that I am on the right track with having lots of classroom discussion — her comments certainly seemed to indicate that the amount of discussion going on was appropriate and significant.
>
> I am also aware that some students need more structure and can't remember everything that was discussed. When a test comes around and the students need to study, there is no record of the discussion to rekindle the thoughts in their mind. On the other side of the coin is the fact that, in some cases, taking rigorous discussion notes has the potential to stifle some of the spontaneity and flow of the discussion. I think it would be appropriate, based on my reflections and listening to the message behind the comment that the student had made, that I develop some sort of sheet that I could have the students use as a template for writing down their thoughts after a discussion has taken place. It could have several questions to catalyze the students' thinking about the discussion. These might include: What are three points that were made in the discussion that will stick with you and why? What did you learn? How did this discussion relate to the main topic we are currently studying?
>
> Also, based on my own thoughts about this activity, I have to ask myself, *what would I do differently next time?* I think that the only sacrifice that I made was some of the very fine subject matter details. In evaluating the projects, I realized that most of the students covered all of the main points; however, some of them did miss some things that I would have liked to see included. In order to deal with this for next time, I could easily prepare a *content sheet* that outlines the points that must be included in the project. As I have retyped this

journal entry, I have also realized that I could very easily turn the content sheet into a checklist that each student must hand in with the project. This would allow them to monitor their own progress as they were completing their project and make them more aware of the specific objectives of the activity.

My final thoughts, for now, concern the writing that I engaged the students in after the presentations had been made. I found that many people wrote that they learned a lot about succession from doing this activity. I want to add a little note to the end of these statements — 'PROVE IT!!!' I like to believe that they did learn it, but I'd be naive to think that they all did. Perhaps the content sheet would help to take care of this. (12 October 1996)

After typing in all the responses to the writing activity, several things come to mind. There are two things that I simply must return to in class. The first is the notion of proof or evidence of their learning. I talked with Peter [Chin] about this last night. His comments, critique and support were, as always, much appreciated and resonate very strongly with my own feelings. We both seem to agree that there has to be more to the learning than, 'It was fun; therefore we learned.' I need to explore this further and focus them a little more on the other reasons for learning rather than simply being engaged in the activity because it was fun. The second issue is that one student had made remarks about another student's presentation. To me, that goes against what I thought we were about as a class. I need to address this issue in the next class.

My plan of action, then, is to raise these issues with the class and then negotiate what to do about them. Hopefully, this will show them that in a class that is founded upon a positive learning environment, problems can be solved with negotiation between me and individual members of the class. The second is that I learn from them. I want to bring up that I noted that Student 16 chose to include an interview to demonstrate her understanding of succession, and that I thought it was an excellent technique that I will use in the future. The final point to bring up is that I find these writing exercises useful because they allow me some insight into how individual students learn and also their misconceptions about the way they see things working. For example, in one project I noted that the student had written that the lichen turned into trees. (13 October 1996)

I've now asked the same class to continue to write about the experience. They are completing the stem 'Doing this activity was fun, but it helped me to learn because . . .'

I've told them a few things today — one was about the impressions that I got from their responses. Another was about my concern for the actual learning that took place. We also talked about the negotiation aspect of what we were doing in class. I read a few quotes from several projects to highlight some things I thought were significant. This sparked some great comments and discussion about *why* it helps to learn that way. I'm now hoping to get right inside their heads to see what they see as good learning behaviours. Perhaps that is where I will go next. They certainly seem to take well to writing. The next issue is to deal with number 1 and 2 from the previous journal entry (i.e., proof/evidence of their learning).

Based on the silence, and the tongues sticking out while they are writing, I think they are really into this exercise.

[Later] I just got the writing from them and have scanned it . . . It looks very promising. I will have to type it into a file and present it to Brian to get his reaction. (15 October 1996)

Brian is one of several colleagues with whom I meet regularly during the school year to act as critical friends for each other. We often discuss what new things we are trying in our classes, what issues are really pressing us, or even what resources we have seen or developed that we think the other might be interested in. In this case, I was hoping that he would be as excited about the following data that I recorded on 15 October 1996 as I was.

Students' responses to the stem, 'Doing this activity was fun, but it helped me to learn because . . .'

. . . I had to think about it and read over the textbook and tried to understand it and then I could write my story. That was help me a lot. I thought I knew succession but when I was doing this activity I knew more than I knew before. (Student 5)

. . . information was presented in a large variety of ways. You have to think about your topic to present it visually and creatively. It's much easier to learn when information is being thrown at you from different directions. You understand all of the topics, not just your own. Going up to the front of the class and reading a poem or singing a song you wrote is a great way to overcome self-consciousness. It's harder for one student to put another down because everybody is doing something original. It's impossible to get bored or inattentive. You really have to have an understanding of your topic and think about it a lot. Note-taking sucks. This way, you learn whether you want to or not, because of the wide range of presentation methods. During a long, six-period day, its great to learn in a relaxed atmosphere for a while to keep our brains from imploding under the pressure. Eased daily stress. It was really interesting to see everyone's creative side, and it gave me new ideas and options for future projects. If any student goes into a class like this with an open mind, they'll come out with a full mind. It's also really cool to have a teacher who doesn't do everything 'by the book.' Happy students aren't hostile students. Its cool how everyone was attentive and helped each other (e.g., back-up singers for the song). It's like other people describing your thoughts back to you. (Student 13)

. . . the poem that I did required me to view a broad range of ideas on secondary succession. Because I really had to sit down and think about what I was doing, the ideas became clearer and made more sense. I looked at every word (almost) in the succession section of my textbook looking for ideas to make a rhyme. By doing so, I took in more information that I would have if I had just been assigned to read the chapter. This activity gave me a chance to learn about something in a way that I liked. I learn more from doing fun projects like this than sitting in class and taking down notes. This activity made me look at secondary and primary succession. I had to read each part on succession very carefully to decide on what would be the best succession to make my poem about. (Student 12)

. . . a real student who knows what a natural succession is and how it did happen. Especially during a disaster. I think my activity wasn't really good because I didn't really understand what to do, and I hope to do my best next time. [just joined the class] (Student 17)

. . . we learned about many things. Example — when we prepared song about natural succession. That's very fun. But we learned about natural succession because when we write song we think about natural succession very carefully and when we do that we memorize that during we don't know. However this activity is acting. When we do this activity, first we think about that and we apply that using poem, writing, etc. . . . so this was very fun but we can learn many things. [S2 includes a diagram of things] (Student 2)

. . . it helped me to learn because of many kind of ways which are poem, story, picture, comic and creative. We get to read textbook science knowledge but it is too boring and we never remember. Activity is easy to understand and we never forget. So it is more utility. And I studied for long time. I could compare to other students present through this activity. (Student 3)

. . . I could understand easier. I can't understand when I read something. But when I look some picture, cartoons, or some other stuff, I understand many thing. When I do this, some parts are I can't understand but other people shows their works and tell the story of the work and then I understand what I can't understand. So I want continue this way to work. (Student 4)

... I, like a lot of people, am pretty visual. Whatever I see that is presented visually, for example a picture, sticks in my mind a lot more easily than a page of notes. However, when I was actually thinking of a creative way to do my activity, I had to broaden my options, so I would be sure that no one else would do the same presentation as me. In doing this, one really has to understand, and turn the ideas over and over in your head, until they come out smooth and presentable, kind of like a milkshake in a blender. Once you have these ideas, you have to make sure the people you are presenting to understand what you're talking about. Seeing your work through other's eyes really helps in the way you carry the point across. It is very important that you understand your subject totally before you teach it to other people. (Student 8)

... during the presentations, everyone displayed their knowledge of succession in different ways, using different examples and mediums. Doing my own project, I had to read about succession and think of examples of how it works. Everyone took, in a sense, the role of a teacher in doing this — having to explain to you and the class what succession is. And since the best way to learn and enforce your learning is to teach, we all benefited from this experience. Personally, making my collage helped me to see how succession is part of everything in our natural world. When I saw a picture of rocks once covered by ocean, I realized that was the result of succession that hadn't been mentioned in the textbook. Yesterday I biked in the Gatineau Hills and noticed that there were trees growing on patches of soil on rocks. I said to myself, 'Hey, that's succession!' I knew that I had learned from this assignment because I usually forget what I learn in science. (Student 6)

... by giving us the freedom to choose an idea or a creative way of presenting something, the idea must be in sync with the actual project. This helps us because not only is it proving to Mr Featherstone that we understand the project, but we're proving it to ourselves that we understand the material. Also, when we are given freedom, it motivates us because we feel good when we see the final product of something we worked really hard on. Also, it motivates me when I see the great response from our teacher, indeed, making it easier to work in class and on other projects. (Student 11)

... by giving us the freedom to choose any way of presenting the information, it allows us to choose the method which best fits us. The first day we received the project I almost immediately decided what to do. But, when I tried to use the idea it didn't turn out very well. And so I experimented with other ideas. In total I probably spent only one third of the time producing the final part. The other two thirds of the time was spent toying with ideas. This was no waste of time though, because every time I started a new idea, more information was taken from the topic. This, in turn, greatly improved the final result. Reading the final product didn't teach me the most; the majority of information was taken from the process itself. The most important aspect of my specific product was the humour. By making a parody of a cook book, it allowed me to learn much better. Another important fact is that this project kept my attention. I suffer from ADHD and this project was so fun and easy, that it never became boring. (Student 10)

... it showed me the best way I can understand something and how good a job I can do when I understand something to my full potential. By giving us a wide variety of choice, it showed me the easiest way that I can learn something fully. In the future when something like this comes up again I will know which way would be the best for me to understand and, therefore, be able to do a reasonably good job on the activity. This serves as a representation of the pictures we have in our mind about succession, and the way that we represent them shows how fully we understand the subject. To write my song, I had to find the right words to be able to get the message across as well as keeping the same beat to the song from which I changed the lyrics. I had to fully understand the project to get these two things across. (Student 7)

... in order to explain natural succession through creative things, we really had to fully understand it beforehand. It also made me learn a lot, because I had to think a lot about natural succession and how it works. By turning this assignment into a fun one, I was more eager to do it and try to do my best in it, and maybe that's why it helped me to learn. Also, when trying to explain a concept like natural succession, I often have to relate to other things (like the glacier to a conveyor belt) and that really helps me to get a deeper understanding of it. It helped us to learn by seeing other people's views on natural succession. (Student 16)

... it gave me the freedom to create something that I could call my own. Also it gave me a visual reference in my mind that I don't think I will forget. I understand it a lot better than I did at the start. That's because I saw many presentations that explained what succession was. Everybody had a different way of looking at succession but got the same important points across to everybody. So, that's how it helped me to learn. (Student 14)

. . . I wanted to find a way that would make the process of succession very clear in my head. I am a tactile learner and therefore learn and retain information best by actually thinking up an idea and then creating it into a material form. I like to work with my hands for three reasons. I enjoy creating things, I learn from my work, and the final product is very rewarding to see. When I found out that I had Attention Deficit Hyperactive Disorder two years ago I was asked to attend a study and work skills course at Turnbull. This was where I found out that I was, in fact, a tactile learner. They taught me many skills as to how I could use this to my advantage. Working with my hands keeps me concentrated and interested which is very important in my case. (Student 9)

. . . it made me bring all the information together and to process it into stages because that is what my diorama was about. It presented different stages in which we could look at it and how they all linked together in one big process of succession. We have to be able to fully understand it to make a presentation because all of the pieces have to fit together to make it complete. (Student 18)

. . . it made me think about this topic. When I first learn of it, I had no clue what was going on. Then I went back and read it again and thought how am I going to present it. Also, this way of learning is more interesting and it also gave me an option of how am I going to learn this about this topic. When I write or copy notes off the board, I don't really think about them, because I don't have the time to think when I copy the notes. So this way it makes learning a lot easier. (Student 19)

. . . not only did we have to fully understand the topic but we had to display it so that other people would have a better understanding of the topic too. This made it fun as well as educational. It also helped me learn more about natural succession by seeing other people's views on the subject. I think I will also remember natural succession better now than if we had just taken notes or answered questions. (Student 1)

After my meeting with Brian, I noted several points in my journal:

Brian and I talked for about forty minutes about things that have been going on lately. We did manage to talk about the data that I was collecting with the students in the class, and he offered some excellent suggestions, as well as reinforced some of the things that I was thinking.

I told him my thoughts about what I had received and the fact that many students in the first round of the writing had said that they learned a lot. His response was something along the lines of, 'But can they prove it?' I showed him the section in my journal that indicated that that was exactly what my first reaction was. From there he gave me the caveat that I must watch what I am doing in terms of being a younger teacher. He mentioned that in some ways it all comes back to content. Even if I give them an open-ended test where they are to write about what they learned about succession, they still have to know the content to succeed. I agreed, and we talked about the blend of traditional thinking and new approaches. I have to blend them both to ensure that I cover the material but, at the same time, I need to make sure that my students enjoy what I am doing, and that I enjoy what I am doing. He also mentioned that when he has had students create cartoons in the past, he has had them submit a required text of explanation with the project. I definitely want to work this in some-where. Some of the projects that I had received were creative, but there wasn't enough explanation accompanying them. (16 October 1996)

What Did I Learn from This?

I can draw several important conclusions from critically reflecting on my own teaching with the help of my students. It seems appropriate to begin by stating my own personal beliefs about the significance of this work and how it has influenced the way that I view teaching and learning. When people talk about learning from experience, there is an immediate connotation that the learning involves a negative experience. Whether it be related to classroom management or teaching techniques, there is no doubt that some very significant learning occurs in negative situations. What is not always brought to light is the significance of learning that occurs in positive experiences. This conversation-about-learning with my students has shown me some of the potential for learning in experiences where little goes wrong. I could have studied my own teaching without my students' input, yet my insights in this experience depend heavily on the students' voices. Aldous Huxley is reported to have said, 'Experience is not what happens to you; it is what you *do* with what happens to you.' It is not enough to have experience. One must attend to what the experience really says, being conscious of the reframing that makes the experience significant. To me, this is the true learning and understanding. Critical friends — whether they be school colleagues, mentors, or your own students — can be invaluable in exploring the learning in our experiences of teaching.

Learning from the Positives and the Not-So-Positives

I have learned that I must continue the type of work I describe here. There are many reasons, including the valuable insights gained into each student's learning style. The entire experience was well worth the effort for all of us. The students seemed to like the fact that, when I asked them to write, I was writing too. Some students expressed the view that it makes the writing appear important if I am writing with them. They seem to be saying that it creates a sense of community in the classroom.

I am eager to do this exercise again. The students liked it, and they seem to agree that they would like to do it again for some other area of our science studies. Many expressed interest in wanting to do it again so that they could improve and use another idea. Most teachers are eager to see students intrinsically motivated to learn and to improve their performance. I am happy to say that I can see the desire in my students to do better.

There are several changes I would make to the way I taught this concept. I would definitely include a content sheet that was developed into a checklist so that each student could monitor the significant points on the list. I would also like to introduce this activity earlier in the year. The way the group has interacted since that day has been phenomenal. I have noticed that in certain assignments they automatically assemble themselves into relatively homogenous cooperative learning groups. They automatically engage in peer teaching activities when there is new vocabulary to be learned. They have accepted not only more responsibility for their own learning, but also some responsibility for learning by others in the class.

Suggestions for Others Interested in this Type of Work

Writing about this episode has been an excellent teaching and learning experience for me. I have worked hard to set up an appropriate classroom atmosphere in which my students may succeed and have their voices heard. This activity worked well for the class I chose, and there were many factors contributing to its success. This is the only class in which I have tried this activity, and so I still don't know how well it would work to engage all my classes to this depth. Starting small is a good idea, for one class can give you more than enough 'food for thought.'

I am aware that the experience that my students and I were writing about was a positive one. In the future, I would like to explore my students' reflections on a negative classroom event or episode. My feeling is that it would be more risky to focus on the negative, so it might be wise to start with the positive and then move towards the negative. An example might be a class that results in puzzled, uncomfortable looks from the students. At that point, writing might be about what was still troubling them with the concepts being studied. This might yield insights into conceptual difficulties and individual learning styles that you may not have taken into account in your teaching.

As I conclude this chapter, I am increasingly aware of the positive contributions to my teaching and learning, and to my finding my own voice as a beginning teacher, by the following individuals who are my 'critical friends.' Many thanks are due to Chris Miedema, Brian Storosko, Peter Chin, Dawn Bellamy, Hugh Munby and Tom Russell. Finally, it is clear now that this phase of my development as a teacher would never have happened without my students' cooperation and willingness to take risks. I have been reminded just how important it is that one does not underestimate the value of creating a forum for listening to students' voices. I found messages from my students at two different levels. On the one hand, the messages were quite obvious, as when several of my students told me directly that they have ADHD and thus are tactile learners. On the other hand, the smallest comment triggered a domino effect in my thinking about how to improve my teaching. For example, the student who said, 'You don't think that the only way we learn is if we are taking notes,' caused me to think critically about what made the discussion so powerful and useful to the students in terms of their learning. This led me to the conclusion that, while I should continue this type of classroom activity, I should also create a method for using these discussions to their maximum potential. Thus I decided to develop a discussion summary sheet. I am certainly not the first to think about this, but there is something special about being able to say that my decision is based on what I have learned from my students.

Chapter 10

Voices of Critical Friends Reflecting on Teaching and Learning Experiences

Peter Chin, Derek Featherstone and Tom Russell

Overview

This chapter presents the voices of a beginning teacher (Derek, a first-year teacher at the time of the data presented here) in conversation about teaching with two teacher educators (Peter and Tom) who worked closely with him during his teacher education program. Earlier versions were presented at several conferences in 1996, and we include our final version here for several reasons. We want to demonstrate the potential for continuing conversation between teacher educators and those they teach in pre-service programs. The growing access of teachers to electronic mail is an important new resource that permits new teachers to share their voices with each other as well as with teacher educators. We also want to demonstrate to those learning to teach that working in teacher education programs can be just as complex and challenging as teaching in elementary and secondary schools. We hope that this chapter demonstrates that teacher educators who support and encourage the development of new teachers' voices also need to develop their own voices and share them in appropriate ways with those learning to teach.

Introduction

We began working together in January 1994 when Derek and Peter joined Tom at Queen's University in Kingston, Ontario. Derek was beginning his pre-service teacher education courses after an extended sixteen-week practicum in a secondary school, and Peter was beginning his appointment as a teacher educator. Tom and Peter were the science methods instructors for the program in which Derek was enrolled. Working together in this instructor–pre-service teacher relationship established the foundation for the collegial relationship that exists today. As Derek moved into his first year of teaching, we made a commitment to continuing our intensive dialogue about our teaching and learning by taking on the role of being 'critical friends' for each other.

Serving as critical friends involves much more than verbally praising what we see as good teaching practice. Two years of collaboration in the context of an experience-intensive teacher education program established a community in which the three of us recognize that we share many common values about what constitutes good teaching and learning. We also believe that improving our practice can only be accomplished through critical reflection, and thus we share a strong commitment to self-study. We agreed to engage in three-way self-study by sharing interpretations and reflections about our teaching and learning experiences. This chapter explores how we move beyond congratulations and challenge each other on issues that surface through studying our teaching practice.

The structure of this chapter mirrors the process that we went through in our collaborative work. We begin with three 'individual pieces' that outline pressing issues each of us is attempting to address in day-to-day teaching. In November, Derek began to speak of Peter and Tom's messages serving as 'lighthouses' in the fog of the first year of teaching. Then, in January, he coined the term 'paper lighthouses' to refer to the broad goals of teaching that he was naming for himself and posting on paper in his office. The three of us now use this term freely, as noted in the conversations shared in this chapter.

The chapter continues with a section written together to explore the collective sense gained in working together on this collaborative project. Excerpts from electronic mail exchanges and transcripts of conversations we audiotaped at several points during the year are used to illustrate how self-study in a community of adult learners has enabled each of us to develop as an educator in ways that would not be possible had we worked independently. To borrow a common phrase, the whole is greater than the sum of its parts. The chapter ends with an analysis of the continuous nature of this collaboration, as the collective sense achieved serves as a springboard into further self-study that is enriched by our common understandings.

Derek's Perspective

Like all teachers, the plans I make are directly related to the ideals that I try to live in my practice. These ideals are based on my past teaching and learning experiences. Although these ideals were in place on the first day of school in September 1995, as I began my first year of teaching, it was not until part way through Christmas holidays that I was able to engage in three-way self-study as deeply as I would have liked.

I focused on two broad goals that guide my teaching. They relate to how I see science education in terms of understanding course material rather than memorizing it. I try to teach using strategies and methods that encourage my students to understand, although I do know that there are times that I see myself doing things that foster memorization. Perhaps this is the reason that I wish to examine my teaching practices with this contrast in mind — I see and feel the need for improvement in this area so that my teaching is more regularly consistent with my beliefs.

These goals are based on my prior experiences as a person learning to teach. The pre-service teacher education program I undertook consisted of sixteen weeks teaching in a secondary school, followed immediately by sixteen weeks of education courses, and ending with another 16-week teaching practicum. I found this to be extremely beneficial to my own learning to teach — I saw educational theory as directly relevant to what I had just experienced first-hand in the classroom. This forms the basis for my focus on understanding versus memorizing, and the strategies that I use to facilitate this understanding.

I try to set up classroom experiences for my students so that more meaningful interaction can occur in discussions about the activities in which they have just participated. Actively engaging my students in these sorts of activities which lead them towards the objective of the lesson is crucial to effective learning. To me this is more conducive to understanding than simply 'telling' my students about the concept as it provides context for the discussion. The 'experience before theory' premise of my teacher education program serves as a model for teaching my students science. Of course, setting up experiences like this cannot happen in all classes, all the time, for all concepts, but I do try to address it as often as I can.

With those goals articulated and in place, I began to teach and examine my practice. I started strongly in September, but by the middle of October I was sleeping little more than four hours a night. I simply could not make our trialogues a priority and still survive the rigours of my first year of teaching. After the Christmas break and some valuable time spent with Tom and Peter, I returned to teaching with a firm vision of what I wanted to accomplish in my classroom teaching practice. Collaborative self-study was at the forefront of my mind once again.

Our face-to-face meeting in January renewed my commitment to engaging in trialogue in order to help each other as much as possible in the role of 'critical friend.'

The trialogue that followed in the next four weeks proved to be essential as I pursued the goals that I had developed for my teaching and my students' learning. Peter and Tom have helped me in many ways, and I look forward to their continued involvement. They support my efforts to encourage understanding when I have students who blatantly tell me that they get good marks by memorizing (not in my class, they don't). They challenge me to look at things that I sometimes take for granted. Most important, as I exchange thoughts with them on their work with pre-service teachers, I am continually reminded to hold on to my ideals and not compromise my beliefs as an educator.

Peter's Perspective

As we take this opportunity to pause and reconstruct our personal and collective understandings of our trialogue conversations, I find it almost impossible to actually identify which ideas, terms, and concerns were actually mine. This is not to say that I didn't have any concerns, because I did have several. What I am trying to say is that through the process of our dialogues and trialogues (both in person and electronically) my understanding has synthesized and 'decompartmentalized' our individual concerns and reframed them as collective ones. Thank goodness for journal notes and logged electronic mail messages because they provide the only artifacts of 'ground zero.'

Two important, and interrelated, issues that emerged in my own teaching this year can be best characterized as 'balancing fish and fishing' and 'getting them to carry the ball.' These issues are not new, but have been recurring themes both in my earlier life as a high school teacher, and in my new life as a teacher educator. They have surfaced with a vengeance this year due to our tripartite efforts at critical friendship, as well as through my own work in the Fall with John Loughran (Monash University) who was here for the term. Undoubtedly, his work with me and with Tom has been influential in the directions that our mutual conversations have taken. These critical friends have served as catalysts for me to re-articulate my beliefs and to re-examine how my actions support, deny, and contradict them.

In the constant self-examination of what I am attempting to do with pre-service teachers, I am guided by an old proverb that goes something like this: 'If a person is given a fish they can eat for a day, but if someone is taught how to fish they can eat for a lifetime.' This balancing act that I try to achieve is a recognition of my perceptions of long-term and short-term goals in my work with pre-service teachers. The long-term goal in my teacher education practice is teaching them how to fish, but I also recognize the pre-service teachers' initial concerns of wanting the goods (i.e., the fish, pre-packaged and ready to eat). My early experiences working with pre-service teachers have also illuminated the fact that there is a broad range of 'readiness' within a class and that, in the process of teaching people for the long term, they may not be as receptive because their more immediate concerns of the upcoming practicum take precedence in their thinking. Pushing the metaphor a bit, there is little gained when teaching a starving person how to fish. Somehow, they need to be supplied with enough fish so that their immediate concerns are met, and they can concentrate on the long-term goal of learning how to fish.

The second issue has to do with who is carrying the ball. More specifically, what is my own role within the classroom and how do I see the pre-service teachers contributing to the process of learning to teach? I recognize that I do play a role in helping to meet the short- and long-term goals of the pre-service teachers. However, I am but one actor who is part of a large supporting cast. To continue the fishing analogy, I do not see myself as the only person who has knowledge about how to fish, nor am I the only fish supplier available. I believe that the more I can get the pre-service teachers to carry the ball, the more they will personally benefit from the experience. This year I have realized, painfully at times, that just because I want to have the class spend more time carrying the ball doesn't necessarily mean that they will. Much tension has developed in the class because a group of people in the room throw the ball back, and tell me that they don't want it! Thus, I have been focusing my attention on ways of encouraging the class to *want* to carry the ball, and to see the value that this has within their own professional development.

Tom's Perspective

Peter Chin and Derek Featherstone became significant parts of my professional life at the same time, in the Winter Term of the 1993–94 academic year. Peter joined the Faculty of Education and began teaching secondary science methods courses parallel to my own. Derek arrived from a term's teaching experience and became a teacher candidate in courses that both Peter and I were teaching. Within a month, the people Peter and I shared in our teaching were telling us that we were sending similar 'basic messages' about science and the process of learning to teach. By the end of the term, Derek had noticeably demonstrated that he understood in a very deep way what Peter and I were attempting to do. He assumed the leadership role in his cohort's production of a book that recognized and celebrated their initial term of teaching experience and their term's study of science teaching methods and issues. My reaction, quite literally, was 'I have been waiting sixteen years to see beginning teachers write this way,' and producing such a book has now become part of the Queen's–Waterloo program tradition.

In many ways, 'the rest is history.' In the two years since Peter and I first taught side by side, with Derek enrolled in both our classes, I have come to take for granted their presence in my professional life. They share my basic commitments to self-study of teaching and other forms of critical reflection on personal teaching practice. They seem to share most of the fundamental values that I have retained as my teaching took many different forms. Although I never get it right and always find it very difficult, I believe it is essential to model what I preach. When I began working with pre-service teachers, they had every reason to be puzzled, for I had taken to heart the conclusions of six history teachers who studied their own teaching: They 'talked too much,' and they found it 'almost impossible to change.' So how could I 'preach' less teacher talk in any way other than talking less? As one of my earlier students put it, halfway through the course, 'Why didn't you tell us you weren't going to tell us?' As I listened to my students returning from two-week teaching placements, I devoted more and more attention to what they were learning from experience and how I could help focus and advance that learning. Schön's (1983) *The Reflective Practitioner* was just what I needed to move me forward, and I became increasingly interested in having people take charge of their own professional development as teachers. But this is never easy for everyone. Some who enter a teacher education program are 'hooked' on letting others do their learning for them. Not Peter and Derek!

As a teacher educator (chemistry–physics), my broadest goal is to provide challenging class experiences and discussions that will encourage people to move forward in their teaching of science. When I taught physics in a secondary school in 1991–92 and 1992–93, I spread students out from 50 to 90 using a marking scheme that any teacher would recognize. In pre-service methods classes, the mark can only be Pass or Fail, but the individuals are again spread out before me. John Loughran observed and discussed with me all my classes in the Fall term of 1996, reaffirming my aim to have people understand and learn from my teaching, using their experiences in my class to guide the experiences they create for their future students. Peter is always there as a partner who understands. Derek has played a remarkable role by listening to my descriptions of long- and short-term 'dilemmas,' giving 'names' that turn my goals into 'paper lighthouses' that we can relate across the teaching the three of us do.

Beginning the Conversations

At the outset, we were quite aware of the fact that our commitment to beginning and maintaining the trialogue would be difficult in light of the exigencies of our daily lives. As a first year teacher, there would be times during the term where keeping in touch with Tom and Peter was probably the last thing on Derek's mind. In addition, there would also be times during the term where Tom and Peter would be traveling the province to see teacher candidates during their practicum rounds. For these reasons, it was decided that using electronic mail would be the best way of sustaining the dialogue. These electronic conversations would be supplemented by scheduling times where the three of us could get together for face-to-face discussions. Of course, this would be easier for Tom and Peter who are two doors away from each other, whereas Derek is two hours away. During the Fall of 1995, both Peter and Tom were able to arrange their schedules for an individual visit to see Derek, and in the new year Derek was able to make two visits to Queen's for group meetings. As it turned out, this chapter is not lacking in the availability of data since we have transcripts of the group conversations and over a hundred logged electronic messages. What follows are excerpts from the data that illustrate the nature and depth of the interactions upon which we reflect, and in which we challenge each other about our teaching practices.

Our Emerging Collective Understanding

For purposes of this chapter, we have identified four 'threads' within our conversations that are indicative of the kind of dialogues that we were engaging in throughout the September 1995 to March 1996 period. These threads illustrate how certain electronic messages served as catalysts for ongoing conversations. As well, careful examination of the messages provides glimpses of how ideas within each thread manage to converge into a larger unifying theme. The four threads are: 1) experience before theory, 2) anyone can buy a textbook, 3) sliding into the swamp, and 4) different contexts, similar issues.

Experience before Theory

These excerpts from e-mail exchanges arise as a result of Derek thinking about how he is and is not setting up experiences for his students in order to provide the opportunity for more effective learning. It was early in his first year of teaching, and he was working hard to 'keep his head above water.' A phone call to Tom on 4 October helped him refocus his teaching to listen to the voices of his students. He describes some of the results in his initial message and then he and Peter discuss the issues further. Tom's absence from the later exchanges is due to one of the pitfalls of electronic messages — specifically, if one forgets to 'cc:' everybody, then some people are inadvertently left out of the loop. In retrospect, a small LISTSERV would have been more useful in ensuring that our messages were distributed and logged.

> **Date: Thu, 5 Oct 95 04:28:39 UT**   **From: Derek**
> **To: Peter, Tom**
> The issue was raised in Chem class that denying early practical experiences was not something that they liked. They wanted to do experiments right at the start of the year. I was not doing things the way that I would really like to do them. I would like to create experiences for my students that give them something to attach meaning to — like the QW [Queen's–Waterloo] program does. So, being conscious of this, today I made some changes in the way that I am doing the Grade 10 course. In light of the experience before theory issue, I decided to take my Grade 10 class outside for a game. It was a simple ecology game called 'Oh, Deer!' It is a population growth simulation that brings in many concepts — ones that we haven't covered yet. There is still more to do in the game, and more follow up, but from what I could tell, a large number of them have met some of the objectives already. One of the students recording the data came up to me and said 'Sir! The population is evening out — it is close to this value every time!!!' Other students noticed the same thing. One of the students came up to me and said, 'Sir, this is the best science class I've ever had.' If I can get one student to say that in each course, once a year, I will be happy . . . *Derek*.

> **Date: Thu, 05 Oct 95 05:11:05 EDT**   **From: Peter**   **To: Derek**
> As for the early experiences issue, I'm not too sure about this one. Doing labs for the sake of doing labs, without purpose, or any background

with which to make sense of the lab seems counter-productive. How do we get 'less interaction with apparatus, and more interaction with ideas?' What's the point of mixing chemicals if we have no understanding of why these chemicals are doing what they are doing? In fact, I may push you a bit here by asking: Is learning to teach science the same as learning chemistry?? Teaching is definitely something that is best learned while immersed in the context, but is the same said for chemistry? Are there ways of drawing on their prior experiences and relating them to chemistry? The 'Oh, Deer!' example is an excellent activity to teach about limits to population growth and carrying capacity, and can definitely be done as part of the learning process (with a bit of prior knowledge). Can we do the same in chemistry? I would think it could be possible in some instances. I would argue that in these instances, there has to be some necessary background information in place before they can get to the 'ah hah!' of the activity. In your message you speak about why you aren't doing more 'learning from experience' in your classes, but I guess I'm asking whether this can realistically be the case in all disciplines, for all topics? Something to think about. Cheers. *Peter*

Date: Fri, 6 Oct 95 05:11:46 UT   From: Derek   To: Peter
As far as the 'experience before theory' issue goes — I don't think I was completely clear in what I had written, and I do agree with what you are saying about it. I don't think that learning to teach and learning chemistry are completely parallel, but they can be pretty close. In a sense, I was not completely immersed in experience without any theory either. I did have the week curriculum course in August before I went to teach and I did have several years of experience within the context (just in a different role — as a student). So, no, I don't think I would leave them completely in the dark on the theory issue — there is some required background knowledge. The 'Oh, Deer!' game was not a case where I was introducing all of the concepts through the game. There were some experiences from that game that I have already used / am using / will use with them in the follow-up. I looked at it as a significant experience to which the students can attach meaning in that and future lessons.

As far as the chemistry goes, which seemed to be more related to the point you were making, again, I agree with you — there is SOME background knowledge that is required before the experiences in order to make them meaningful . . . What I see [as] the problem with what I was doing is that basically a month had gone by, with no labs. In a way, it was like denying a consecutive BEd student some of the experiences needed. In the first 18 weeks of Education courses, only 3 [weeks are devoted to] experience, and even they [come] 6 weeks into the term. I need to find the balance between 'telling' them some of the basics that they need to know so they are not going through the experience with blinders on, but still making it so the experience is meaningful and has the potential to create some coherent linkages between the lab and 'lecture' component of the course . . . *Derek.*

Initially this exchange began when Derek wrote of the contrast between two consecutive days' teaching. The issue of experience before theory has been a focal point for Derek because of the obvious parallel to the structure of the teacher education program in which he worked with Tom and Peter. Much discussion surrounds this issue as Derek and Peter challenge each other to see just how far the parallel between the two contexts of learning science and learning to teach science can be stretched.

Anyone Can Buy a Textbook

After a trialogue discussion on 5 January, Derek decided to share some of his specific goals with Tom and Peter in order to permit them some clearer insight as his critical friends. In these e-mail excerpts, we see that this pushes both Tom and Peter to think about their own use of texts in their past, present, and future teaching.

> **Date: Sat, 6 Jan 96   From: Derek   To: Peter, Tom**
> **Subject: More thoughts on my teaching & paper lighthouses . . .**
> I just want to let you both know the direction I am taking — what my paper lighthouses are — for the next while. As well, I want to spell each one out a bit, just to articulate my thinking and reasoning behind these particular lighthouses.
> ANYONE CAN BUY A TEXTBOOK — This is one of my top priorities. There are times this past term when I have relied too heavily on the material in the textbook in order to save time. I KNOW that I do have to do that in order to survive, I just want to try and be less reliant on the textbook. I want their primary resources in the class to be their minds and me, and have the text as a back-up. Like I said, I know that I need the textbook to be there for me, and I anticipate I will have to use it as a crutch SOMETIMES — I just want to make sure that I establish a better balance and try to ensure that they come away feeling like they do know quite a bit, and that all knowledge is not contained in textbooks. *Derek.*

> **Date: Tues, 9 Jan 1996   From: Tom   To: Derek, Peter**
> **Subject: Some thoughts on Derek's thoughts . . .**
> ANYONE CAN BUY A TEXTBOOK — Your take on this one surprised me, after my time at F__ Secondary School. What do you know about

how they actually use and don't use the text? Do they read it? Is it a place from which you draw problems/questions they have to answer? How does the text relate to the notes they make or you give them? If the text is NOT the source of all knowledge, where is the extra knowledge coming from? Unless it's just 'common sense that we make up as we go,' I assume it has to come from hands-on personal experience. Where and how often do they get that? In short, it's great to want to change the traditional views of the text, but they need evidence to do so. *Tom*

Date: Wed, 31 Jan 96   From: Peter   To: Derek, Tom
Subject: Re: More thoughts on my teaching & paper lighthouses
Anyone can buy a textbook — I recognize what you mean by this. In my own teaching, I used to hand out textbooks as resources, but then rarely used the text at all. So what did I do??? I prepared notes from that textbook, and other textbooks. I prepared worksheets rather than using chapter questions. I can also see how Tom's questions make sense too. Did I really know how often or in what way they used the textbook? Did they use my notes or the textbook to answer worksheet questions? Did they study from class notes and/or the textbook for exams?? Gee . . . I don't really know. I guess the more important issue in taking ownership for your own learning is this — if we don't rely on a text, does that mean we have to rely on the teacher? Cheers, *Peter*

Date: Fri, 2 Feb 96 05:11:40 UT   From: Derek
To: Tom, Peter
Peter, you wrote something in your response to my paper lighthouses regarding the 'anyone can buy a textbook' section that really made me think — you ask a great question at the end that in my mind relates to all of our teaching situations. I think one theme that is common among the three of us is the undergirding desire and belief to have students or pre-service teachers take ownership for their own learning. You ask, 'If we don't rely on a text, does that mean we have to rely on the teacher?' What a perfect question. My initial thoughts go both ways. . . . yes, because we are the ones who can recognize the behaviours of those who take ownership and we can encourage more of the same. No, because I feel that at the start of the process of being in my class, I want them to rely on me for that kind of encouragement, but I also want to wean them off it as things progress. I think that perhaps our education culture has ingrained in most students that they DO rely on the teacher. So perhaps the issue then is not so much of reliance on the textbook, but finding ways to have those students who are looking to the teacher as the 'sage on the stage' move towards [the teacher] being the 'guide on the side.' If they so much want to rely on the 'expertise' of the teacher, then that may be the time to

take advantage of that, when you have their attention (whether they are waiting to be told what to memorize, or they are waiting to be told how to teach concept x, or manage a classroom). Perhaps that is the time where you have to compromise a little and give in. If you don't compromise then, when you know that they are paying attention, then maybe that is the reason resistance comes later as one tries to help the students be more independent. *Derek.*

Date: Mon, 05 Feb 96 21:54:59 EST   From: Peter
To: Derek, Tom
Another quick response. This time a bit of a chuckle at the good old parallels between your teaching of your students, and my teaching of my classes. Your reactions to the 'textbook issue' as it relates to memorizing versus understanding has now got me pondering whether I should go with the textbook next year. Without a textbook, there are some in the class that then expect me to deliver what they want, since I'm the only show in town. I could see the text as a crutch to wean them with. For them, having the 'book with the answers' may be what I need so that they come to realize that they need to experience what the book has to say, not just memorize it. Interesting: by giving them what they want, they will realize that it really isn't what they want or need?? Maybe. Cheers. *Peter*

This exchange resulted from Derek's creating, as a 'paper lighthouse,' the goal of becoming less dependent on the textbook in planning his lessons. Tom's response raised many questions and issues that resulted in Peter and Derek rethinking and reframing their own use of texts in their teaching. As a result, Derek points to parallels between the use of texts as resources in both secondary school science and learning to teach science, as well as the attitudes of the learners in each context. This issue is obviously of great concern to all of us, as we seem to agree that one of the most important, but sometimes under-valued, resources in the classroom is the students themselves.

Sliding into the Swamp

This thread illustrates the cascading effect of how one message prompts a reply, and it is the reply that becomes the catalyst for developing a salient point in our collective understanding. Again, several similarities about how the three of us perceive our roles as teachers are evident in these messages. As an aside, you can notice the large time lag in Peter's response to Tom, which is indicative of the fact that unlike face-to-face conversations, electronic replies can dangerously slip from one's list of priorities. Luckily, his reply was still appropriate and timely.

Date: Fri, 19 Jan 96 03:55:39 UT   From: Derek
To: Peter, Tom
It has been two of the quickest weeks that I have had here at Ashbury. I need to take a minute or two just to sketch out some of my thoughts as to how they have been in terms of my own productivity, and how things are going in my classes, and send them on to the two of you to let you know how my pursuit of my paper lighthouses is going. Overall, my organization has improved. This organization is the cornerstone of how well things are going for me right now. I know exactly where I am headed in all of my courses right now, and that is something that simply allows me to do all of the other things that I want to do. Of course, it is so easy to see it now, having lived in disorganization for four months from Sep to Dec. I knew back then that I had to be organized, but simply knowing it didn't help me to get out of the mess. It was as though I knew that there was a problem, but felt my hands were tied and I couldn't find any ways to solve the problem. I am pleased with my lessons right now. I am working hard with the Bio 11 class to give them the 'SO WHAT?!?' every class. I have had several comments from the members of that class that they are really happy and are pleased with how things have changed. And for now, even though it is still early in the term, I am keeping the pace where I want it. I am asking more of the types of questions that I want in terms of checking their understanding and involving applications wherever I can. I feel that there IS more coherence and continuity in my lessons (and I have had similar indication in my other classes as well . . .).

I am thinking about my teaching right now . . . the nice thing is, having the clean slate for the new term, as well as my organization etc . . . has allowed me to focus more on the things that I *am* doing in the classroom and my lessons in a positive way, rather than focusing on the things that I *wasn't* doing, or *wished* I was doing in the class with my lessons. Must be off to do some things for tomorrow . . . Thanks for listening!!! *Derek.*

Date: 19 January 1996, 06:50:55 EST   From: Tom
To: Derek, Peter   Subject: You're thanking me for listening???
You've got the outline of a paper right there in that note. Nothing missing!! OFF the scale. I'm tempted to say that it had to be this way, Derek — that you had to slide into the swamp before you could see where you had to pick yourself up. I have a hunch that most new teachers keep on sliding — and don't begin to turn around with the intensity and focus you have — because of your 'steel trap mind' and

your willingness to trust us to listen-comment-insult-provoke. THANKS — you don't know just how rich that looks to these eyes!! *Tom*

Date: Thu, 01 Feb 96   From: Peter   To: Tom, Derek
Re: You're thanking me for listening???

Tom, you mention in your message about having to slide into the swamp before you can see where you had to pick yourself up, and that some people just keep on sliding. Many things come to mind for me right now in my own parallel life (with Derek's). How long did I slide? Did I pick myself up or was it John's facilitating that helped me out? Am I out of it yet? I know that this term has been a new experience for me. I could sympathize with your struggles with last year's physics class, but until you live it, one really doesn't grasp the difficulty. As well, even though I've always been 100% behind the premises in your paper last year (They can't do what I'm asking them to do . . . sorry about my memory of that title) . . . it wasn't until this term that I saw it for my own eyes when the concurrents left. Sure, I always noticed differences between the consecutives and the QW last year (which was my first full year where I wasn't just crutching around and planning lessons the night before) but those differences weren't as pronounced. Fortunately, or unfortunately depending on the spin you want to put on it, I didn't have any vocal 'give us the goods' people. It wasn't until this term that I actually had someone put the Faculty Calendar in front of my face and say, 'We haven't done this.' To me, the real crux in my teaching, and maybe in Derek's (?) is how do I achieve/compromise/come to grips with: A) letting the class benefit from my experience, and B) letting the class benefit from their own experience in learning by doing (both in my class and in their own teaching)? What do we mean by benefit? And which of my experiences are the ones that are valued? The most frustrating thing about the last month has been the fact that some people see my value to them based on the fact that I used to be a classroom teacher. Cheers. *Peter*

Date: 1 February 1996, 08:45:13 EST   From: Tom
To: Peter, Derek

No time to read it all and also finish marking papers to return at 10.30. But I've happened on to your 'sliding into the swamp' message, and I have to say it's probably etched into my mind indelibly already. I feel like after 18 years here, someone finally understands — really understands — in the gut — where all teaching has to be understood. Nice one, Tom, maybe that's the problem we are seeing in our two groups — some are *unwilling* to feel teaching in their guts — and want to treat it all as a show-and-tell. I'm still struggling with the issue of the gap between great demos and understanding. Those people just want demos, and to hell with the issue of transfer. Of course, it's the total

neglect of 'transfer' that characterizes the typical school experience —
'spinach is good for you, and you'll never need it again.' Right back
to Derek's student struggling to figure out what to memorize, and how
to cope when the teacher won't tell her. I've noticed a piece of Waterloo backtalk that suggests that if they don't have notes from here,
they'll never remember all this stuff when they get to the classroom in
3 years. Again, they frame it as a memory problem, not as learning
from experience. Do they have notes that they refer to when they
want to remember how to READ?? Do they forget how to read? Do
teachers forget how to teach? THANKS, Peter. *Tom*

Derek's message served as an update about how his teaching had improved this term mainly because of his focus (i.e., paper lighthouse) of
being organized, and this allowed him to spend more time engaging in
ways that promote the kind of learning he wants to have in his classrooms. Tom's supportive response raises the 'swamp' issue (alluding to
one of Schön's analogies) that Peter's message expands upon. Tom's
final response takes the dialogue to a new level when he shares his
interpretation of what Peter's message meant to him, and manages to
show the parallels between 'teaching is in the gut' and 'teaching is
telling.'

Different Contexts, Similar Issues

This final thread provides the most obvious example of how all three
of us manage to see the same issues being paralleled in our own teaching contexts. At first glance, one would wonder aloud as to the value
of a three-way critical friendship comprised of a beginning teacher,
beginning teacher educator, and experienced teacher educator, but our
own work has resulted in a convergence in a more generic understanding of the critical issues in teaching and learning that are prevalent in
all teaching contexts.

Date: Wed, 31 Jan 96 03:51:00 UT   From: Derek
To: Peter, Tom   Subject: update . . .
A significant event today. Extra help session after school with some of
my biology students. One who has been troubled lately by her health,
and two who don't seem to want to do anything but memorize and
have me tell them exactly what they need to know for the test tomorrow. One of the memorizers said to me 'Sir, how come I've always
had 90's in Science before and now that I am here I am failing?' Yeesh,
I hate those. Within the next two sentences she told me that she just

doesn't know what to memorize because the type of questions that I ask are not clear enough. She also said that by not clear enough she meant that she didn't know what I was asking . . . she didn't know what to answer . . . because the questions are not, 'Define XXX,' or 'How many YYYs does it take to ZZZ?' To her and the other memorizers in the class, 'Why is cellulose important to plant cells?' and 'Where is cellulose found in the cell?' are completely different and unrelated questions.

I told her that there is always some memorization, but that the other questions are the thinking questions that require understanding rather than memorization. She replied that that sucked because in the past all she had to do was memorize and she would get good grades. I responded with 'How much of what you studied last year in science do you remember now?' She said 'None. I forgot it all right after the exam.' I said, 'Then I guess you really didn't learn much then . . .' I told her that memorization was not really good learning. She said 'But it gets good grades.' I said, 'Not in my class.' She just didn't seem to get the point that the questions that I ask are designed for thinking rather than memorizing, and that if she intends only to memorize, then she will not succeed as she has in the past.

I don't know if there is anything really there to challenge or push me on, but I needed to share that story with people I knew would understand. It just bugged me, and then, of course, I started to think about what I have done as a teacher that encourages understanding rather than memorization. Of course, I started to doubt myself, and was confronted with the tension of how I am finding my place within my own teaching. I think I have to bring my teaching more in line with the type of assessment that I am doing. I ask these questions that require understanding, but I think I have to do more than that. I know it will be slow, but necessary. It will come. I still feel that I am doing a good job, largely because when I was really bugged about it, I remembered that it is indeed a destreamed world. I am going to focus on concept maps as a way of linking the vocabulary and concepts together. If I don't focus on one strategy I will not be likely to succeed. So then, as far as my paper lighthouses go, I have done well on some, not as well on others, but I feel I am pulling it together. *Derek*

Date: 31 January 1996, 08:39:59 EST   From: Tom
To: Derek, Peter   Subject: Beauty!

Wonderful material, Derek. I've taken the liberty of sending it on to Stefinee. Let me know if I was overly bold. Amazing how your note makes me think about our work here in new ways too! The account of the presentation on science courses and how students reacted left me feeling very excited, and that your career is in exactly the right place. Wherever you go, a solid base of success in your earliest years of science teaching is the keystone to future success. You are getting it, very quickly, and very deservedly. We're having a fascinating time with QW96. Much they run on their own, especially the Monday sessions. Two days ago they ended on, 'How do we shift motivation from extrinsic to intrinsic?' and Peter and I did a 'seamless transition' at the start of his 2 hours with them, giving them scrambled notes and Venn diagrams from PEEL [Project for Enhancing Effective Learning, Melbourne, Australia] and then giving them the Ian Mitchell handout [which is now Chapter 10 in the second PEEL book — Baird and Northfield, 1992]. Never was it clearer to me that the point of each and every one of those PEEL strategies is to *engage* the students more in their learning, to move them past memorization to some greater level of understanding, to create *challenge* (does that have a place among the lighthouses?). The girl who memorizes and forgets so well probably wouldn't recognize challenge when she saw it. Your account made me remember the observation some people make that Biology is more of a foreign language than French! I also wondered if you could make the 'memorization–understanding' issue something for a CLASS to discuss, perhaps in the first 15 minutes that you see them in any week. I'm thinking of 'What do you remember from last week's work? The week before that? What did you memorize? What did you understand — what new ways of looking at the world did you achieve?' This sounds a little phoney as I type, but you get the drift. I go back to my third year of teaching, when being in my second school and third year led me to say all year — as a theme song — that what I cared about was what they would remember in 5 years, not 5 weeks (or 5 days). Just some quick thoughts to thank you for sparking my day, on a day that really needs sparking. Great to hear from you. *Tom*

Date: Thu, 1 Feb 96 00:50:38 UT   From: Derek
To: Tom, Peter   Subject: RE: Beauty!
NO PROBLEM at all Tom, with sending the note on to Stefinee [Pinnegar, Brigham Young University]. I like her idea, and do something similar in order to encourage that sort of thinking. Quite often I'll take a student answer, and ask someone else in the class to explain why the first person gave the answer they did . . . I think it is similar . . . but reading Stefinee's note made me think of something more that I know I will be able to do in the future (perhaps not this year, but definitely in the future . . .). Once I've been through the material at least once, I will know what the students need to memorize and what they have to understand. There definitely is a place for engagement and challenge among the paper lighthouses — I think they are wrapped up there in Bananas (a la PEEL) — but they certainly do need to be made explicit sometimes . . . I wonder how pre-service teachers take to engaging in this issue of memorization versus understanding? I

know how I made meaning of it during my time at Queen's, and how useful a parallel it is to 'Others cannot tell you how' . . . memorization of facts in Science, and an unending desire for some to want to be told how to teach (like learning algorithmic behaviours as a teacher for daily teaching because someone told you to do it . . .) versus understanding how the material relates together (and understanding and questioning your teaching and why you do what you do in the classroom . . .). Perhaps there is something in there that particularly troubles pre-service Science teachers, since in a lot of cases they are quite accustomed to memorization and regurgitation. I love these writing sessions — wish I had time for more as they always seem so productive . . . Always giving me a slightly different spin on things to help me find my place in my teaching . . . *Derek.*

Date: Thu, 01 Feb 96 01:48:31 EST   From: Peter
To: Derek, Tom   Subject: Re: update . . .
Glad to hear that you are still keeping the strain (that's oil well talk about not letting things get slack), Derek. Your memorizing episode is memorable. It sounds to me like you were trying to talk to her about the BIG 'So what?' in your class rather than the day-to-day conceptual, 'So what?' I almost get the impression that she is convinced that succeeding in life is based on her ability to memorize. I wonder whether real life examples would work here. I also wonder whether your situation with her is mirrored in my situation with the small but vocal group in my class. Your comment about bringing your teaching more in line with the kind of assessment you want to do hits the nail on the head, and I think Stefinee's response provides suggestions for doing so. Finally, I do agree that it is a destreamed world . . . especially in the Sahara! Cheers. *Peter*

Date: Mon, 05 Feb 96 21:40:16 EST   From: Peter
To: Derek, Tom   RE: Beauty!
Just a quick response/reaction/epiphany to your message about memorizing versus understanding. This is probably just a repetition of some other things, but I find it a useful way of thinking about it.

SOME OF MY CLASS	THE REST OF THE CLASS
memorizing	understanding
surface learning	deep learning
teaching is in the notes	teaching is in the guts
being told about things	experiencing things

The real kicker is getting people to move from the left to the right. I actually may use these parallels next year . . . and see if it quells some of the 'want' of my 'tricks' to teaching. Cheers. *Peter*

This series of interactions was pivotal in consolidating our collective understanding of the critical issues of teaching and learning that can be found in any teaching context, whether it is a high school science or a university science methods classroom. As we shared critical incidents that were occurring in our own classrooms, it became obvious that we could begin to attach certain labels to the two different kinds of learners that are in our charge. The development of the chart contained in Peter's final message above serves as a basis for constructing the coherence we now see pervading our e-mail and face-to-face discussions.

Consolidation and Continuing Our Conversations

By sharing some of the dilemmas and frustrations in our teaching with each other, and by pushing each other to take our descriptions and interpretations further, we believe that we have arrived at an understanding greater than any of us could have come up with alone. We have come to recognize that many of our discussions highlight the fact that the same issues in teaching and learning permeate all education settings. The four themes illustrated illuminate many of the parallel issues that we need to address when working with students, whether they are in high school or in a teacher education program. The following chart summarizes our thinking about what each of us is trying to accomplish as a teacher.

THOSE WHO WANT TO BE TAUGHT	THOSE WHO WANT TO LEARN
Memorizing	Understanding
Surface learning	Deep learning
Teaching is in the notes	Teaching is in the gut
Tell me about it	Show me and let me do it myself
Extrinsic motivation	Intrinsic motivation
Grades	Pass/Fail
Preparing for the short term	Preparing for the long term
Make the judgment for me	Form own judgment based on experience
Teacher-directed learning	Teacher- and self-directed learning
Basic training	Professional development
Fish	Fishing

These dichotomies serve important roles in our future discussions of classroom practices. It is critical to recognize that our classes will always include some who 'want to be taught' and others who 'want to learn.' Our recent discussions have focused around trying to find specific clues to recognizing where each person can be placed within this framework. Also, we need to find ways of encouraging our students who may seem entrenched on the left side of the chart to begin to make moves towards the right side of the chart. How can we help them see the value of considering learning in a different way? Finally, this chart serves as a new 'paper lighthouse' that we can use critically to evaluate our own teaching.

What are the ways in which we undermine our own efforts by doing things that contradict our goals and beliefs about teaching? As a simple example, it can be a living contradiction to give a lecture on the advantages of learning in small groups. Many would argue that such an objective should be conveyed by opportunities to *experience* learning in small groups. The central issue we continue to strive for in our teaching can be captured in the important phrase, 'Other voices can help you find your own.' For the three of us, this is not the end of our work together as critical friends. Rather, it is the beginning of another cycle of critically engaging in and supporting our mutual efforts to achieve our teaching ideals within our classrooms.

Subsequent discussions within our trialogue and with a wider audience of colleagues at conferences have pushed our thinking further. The 'paper lighthouses' have served not only as a means of critically evaluating our *teaching*, but also as catalysts for critically evaluating our *thinking about teaching*. Rather than seeing the chart as a set of 'either-or' dichotomies between those who want to be taught and those who want to learn, we now see it more as a context-dependent guide for interpreting learner responses. Specifically, we want to understand better the kinds of situations that cause a person to take the stance of 'wanting to be taught' and the kinds of situations where an individual is more likely to take up the challenge of 'wanting to learn.'

Our conference presentations to other colleagues have added welcome new perspectives on our shared experiences, as they have also pointed to the potential value of extending the conversations beyond our trialogue. As well, we plan to broaden the base of our explorations of teaching and learning to include the participation of those we teach, by asking our students to tell us about the ways we enhance or constrain their learning and development as professionals. Through this process of listening to ourselves, to our students, and to other colleagues, our own efforts as critical friends can be extended. The sharing of teaching voices among those who understand each other's goals is an experience that we would recommend to all who seek to improve their teaching.

Note

Earlier versions of this chapter were presented at the meeting of the American Educational Research Association in New York in April 1996, and at the First International Conference on Self-Study of Teacher Education Practices at the Queen's University International Study Centre, Herstmonceux Castle, East Sussex, UK, in August 1996.

References

BAIRD, J.R. and NORTHFIELD, J.R. (1992) *Learning from the PEEL Experience*, Melbourne, Monash University Printing Services.
SCHÖN, D.A. (1983) *The Reflective Practitioner: How Professionals Think in Action*, New York, Basic Books.

Author Index

Subject Index

associate teacher, x, 12, 17, 19, 20, 22, 30, 32, 33, 37, 41, 49, 51, 52, 53, 54, 55, 56, 59, 61, 63, 64, 65, 66, 67, 70, 72, 75, 77, 81, 82, 86, 87, 88, 89, 90, 91, 92, 93, 94, 95, 96, 99, 100, 101, 106, 119

authority, x, 2, 3, 5, 6, 9, 14, 34, 35, 70, 71, 74, 80, 103, 104, 111, 114, 116

challenge, 11, 13, 53, 57, 61, 67, 71, 74, 75, 78, 91, 98, 103, 111, 114, 116, 117, 138, 140, 143, 146, 152, 153, 156

confidence, 3, 4, 9, 10, 12, 13, 29, 43, 44, 62, 64, 69, 70, 71, 80, 84, 87, 89, 115

crisis, 100, 105, 106, 107, 108

critical friend, 35, 106, 120, 121, 122, 129, 134, 136, 138, 140, 146, 151, 156

discipline, 9, 23, 33, 52, 73, 84, 92, 95, 99, 101, 104, 145

experience, ix, x, xi, 1, 2, 3, 4, 5, 6, 7, 8, 9, 11, 12, 13, 14, 15, 16, 18, 21, 22, 27, 29, 30, 33, 36, 37, 38, 40, 41, 42, 43, 44, 48, 49, 50, 51, 53, 54, 55, 56, 57, 58, 60, 61, 63, 64, 66, 67, 68, 70, 71, 74, 76, 77, 78, 79, 80, 81, 82, 83, 84, 86, 87, 88, 89, 90, 91, 92, 94, 95, 96, 98, 99, 100, 105, 106, 107, 108, 109, 110, 114, 115, 116, 117, 118, 120, 122, 123, 124, 127, 128, 131, 134,

135, 136, 138, 139, 141, 142, 143, 144, 145, 146, 147, 148, 150, 151, 155, 156

homework, 10, 11, 23, 25, 26, 30, 37, 78, 90

identity, 81, 82, 117, 119

learning to teach, ix, x, xi, 1, 2, 3, 4, 5, 6, 7, 8, 9, 13, 21, 40, 41, 42, 44, 48, 60, 91, 93, 98, 109, 110, 112, 113, 119, 137, 139, 141, 142, 145, 146, 148

lesson, 2, 8, 10, 12, 22, 24, 25, 27, 29, 35, 37, 38, 49, 50, 51, 52, 54, 55, 57, 61, 62, 63, 64, 65, 66, 71, 72, 73, 74, 75, 77, 83, 84, 86, 89, 90, 92, 93, 95, 96, 99, 101, 104, 107, 111, 117, 139, 145, 148, 149, 150

management, 8, 15, 21, 29, 30, 42, 50, 52, 54, 63, 66, 68, 81, 90, 99, 102, 103, 105, 106, 134

nervous, 12, 49, 63, 66, 67, 70, 76, 82, 86, 88, 89, 95, 113, 117

PEEL, 153, 157

PGCE, 109, 111, 112, 113, 115

plan, 5, 22, 24, 25, 26, 27, 29, 36, 37, 49, 50, 52, 54, 56, 57, 61, 64, 66, 74, 76, 81, 84, 89, 92, 94, 95, 96, 99, 103, 128, 134, 138, 148, 150, 152

POE, 48, 50, 55, 56, 57, 106